P9-DMX-549

HOMESICK

a memoir

JENNIFER CROFT

The Unnamed Press
Los Angeles, CA

AN UNNAMED PRESS BOOK

www.unnamedpress.com

Unnamed Press, and the colophon, are registered trademarks of Unnamed Media LLC.

ISBN: 9781944700942

Library of Congress Cataloging-in-Publication Data is available upon request.

Photographs by Jennifer Croft and Laurie Croft
Cover Design by Jaya Nicely

The Russian poem titled "There are no boring people in this world" by Yevgeny Yevtushenko was originally published in *Tenderness: New Poems*, Moscow, 1962.

This book is a work of creative nonfiction.
Names, identifying details, and places have been changed.

Distributed by Publishers Group West
Manufactured in the United States of America
First Edition

for my sister

We photographers deal in things that are continually vanishing, and when they have vanished, there is no contrivance on earth that can make them come back again.

Henri Cartier-Bresson

A picture is a secret about a secret. The more it tells the less you know.

Diane Arbus

HOMESICK

Remember when I used to make you practice saying words?

I'd say, Repeat after me: Egg, *and you'd lean back ever so slightly like you were about to take off and then go,* AIG! *An emphatic Oklahoman always.*

Although each time for one split second
(German: Augenblick, *literally* blink of an eye,
in blink's *oldest meaning of* starry fleeting gleam*)*
you'd just sit there and wait for my face to tell you
whether you had done it right.

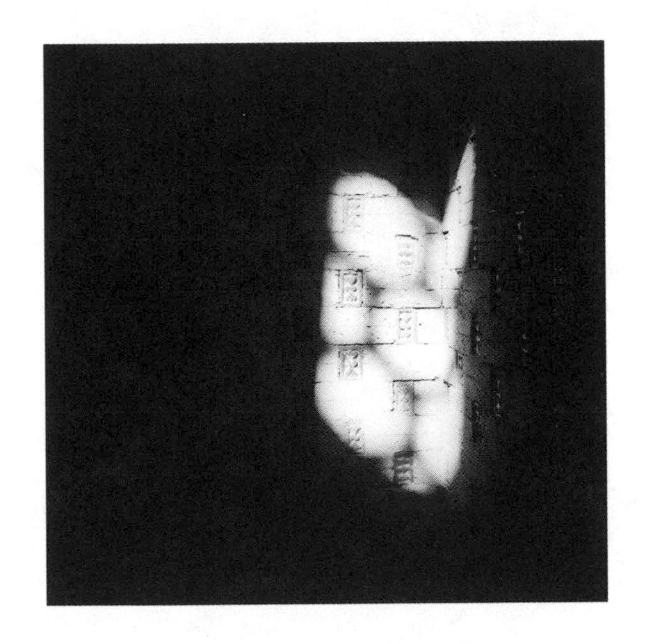

And then I'd scowl, and you would look away.

PART ONE:
SICK

Their mom gets them ready for all the possible disasters that might ever occur

So she reads aloud the headlines from the Tulsa World at breakfast while Amy and Zoe eat their Cheerios. The girls stay quiet while their mother talks, but they don't really listen. All they know is that there is always a disaster happening somewhere. Besides tornados there are earthquakes, and plane crashes, and wars. There is an AIDS epidemic, although neither Amy nor Zoe knows what AIDS is. They only know they are supposed to wash their hands.

There is also the story of the shibboleth, which means when you can't cross the river because you say the words wrong and then get murdered.

When she takes her baths their mom reads them articles from Good Housekeeping. She never ever takes showers because she says she saw a movie one time where the main character got killed while she was taking a shower, and then there was blood everywhere. She likes for the girls to keep her company while she's in the bathtub.

Sometimes she tells family stories. She always tells everyone the one about the crazy neighbor from down the cul-de-sac who shot his family and then hid in the big tree in the backyard. Their dad was off in Stillwater running one of his workshops on geography. So their mom went and picked his rifle up and prepared herself to do whatever was necessary to protect them. She put Amy under the bed and told her to stay there no matter what, and not to make a sound. No matter what, she repeats, and every time she tells the story her voice gets thick there.

Zoe was still a baby and had to be held. Even though she was a baby she could sense that something was wrong because she would not stop crying, and that made you think, says their mother, about those women in the Holocaust who had to smother their own kids so they wouldn't get discovered.

Amy and Zoe know the Holocaust was when the Jewish people all got murdered for no reason and dumped into a big pit in the forest.

So their mother had Zoe in one arm, wailing, and the gun in the other. The police were there already and had him surrounded. They knew this from the TV because even though it was literally right there in their backyard their mom knew she had to stay away from the windows in case a bullet came through. The crazy neighbor kept shooting and shooting and even shot one of the other neighbors who had come over to help the police.

Here their mother pauses and looks around every time she tells the story.

But the man who got shot chewed tobacco. And he happened to be chewing tobacco right then. The bullet went in through his cheek at an angle like this—their mother points to her cheek using her forefinger as a pistol—but instead of going on into his throat and finishing him off it lodged in his tobacco!

Everyone always likes that part, which the girls don't understand because they know that tobacco will kill you too, and besides they see this neighbor all the time sitting out on his porch spitting out his black juices into a big tin pail, skin and bones and ragged looking, that ugly old scar on his face.

But Amy hates the whole story. She can't remember being alone under the bed, but she's heard about it so much she can picture it, so much so that sometimes she has dreams about it: Zoe orbiting around, crying, out of her reach.

In the end, the crazy neighbor shot himself, and then he died.

Even though she knows she's not supposed to, Amy looks forward to tornados

Even in the day the sky gets black, and the streets get empty. The wind pries back the leaves of the silver maple tree, and underneath they gleam.

When it's a tornado watch they don't do it, but when it's a tornado warning, the girls go and get inside the pantry, where they squeeze in among the cans and powders and cardboard boxes and wait until one of their parents says they can come out. The pantry is the only place in the whole house that does not have windows. You have to stay away from windows when a tornado comes because the very thing tornados love best is breaking glass, and if that happens, and you're sitting for example in the bathtub right below the bathroom window, you will almost inevitably get hurt.

When the sirens start, Amy gets them organized. She has developed a system. Each of them is allowed three toys, not more, and Amy is in charge of the flashlight because Zoe might break it. Zoe always dallies over her dolls, feeling guilty for playing favorites. But Amy explains to her how in life you have to make choices, and eventually Zoe always does, although sometimes she tries to hide things in her tiny pants pockets.

When she gets caught she bursts out laughing or into tears depending on Amy's face. She always gets caught. Then Amy quiets Zoe, and they kneel down on the dimpled linoleum, pull the door shut, and wait.

Once the door is closed, Zoe's dolls have conversations. Often they discuss the weather. Amy just listens, lets her own dolls rest, feels her sister's hot quick breaths on her neck. If their electricity isn't out, Amy insists the light be off anyway. Slowly she gets sleepy like she does in the car, and just like when they drive somewhere, Amy, unlike Zoe, would rather just not get there, would rather just keep going, would like it if the warning never expired. Then the pantry door will fly wide open, and all across the top of it the frying pan and the strainer and all the knives will glint and shiver like they want to fall. And their mother will reach down and grab Zoe, and then she'll carry her away.

Do you ever wonder where words come from, Zoe?

The first time Zoe isn't Zoe anymore is on the morning of her preschool graduation

Amy has just finished second grade.

Since their grandma and their grandpa hardly ever come to school, now the girls talk over one another, each hoping to capture their attention. Zoe squawks like the blue jay in the backyard that dive-bombs the cat with its beak, leaving bald spots. Finally their grandpa stoops over, showing all the baldness on his head, and picks her up and takes her to the playground.

In the peace this break affords them, Amy shows their grandma all her work. She has nearly completed a whole spiral notebook, the words resolving into what they mean: squint and butterfly's already butterfly, not simply scratches on the brittle pages, but aloft, like magic.

Their grandma squints and oohs and ahs, until all of a sudden, their grandfather returns.

Amy freezes, eyes wide. She understands without knowing that everything has changed.

Their grandpa says he thinks that Zoe might have bumped her head. Their grandma says, Oh, Zoe, don't be such a baby, then flips another page of Amy's notebook.

Amy glances over at the notebook, sees that all the creatures from her stories have collapsed back into squiggles, lines snapping undone. Splotches over i's and j's bulge hideous, must be mistakes.

Amy knows the worst thing you can do to Zoe is tell her that she's a baby. Often if you do so Zoe howls. Sometimes she throws things.

But now Zoe does nothing. She won't even look back. Amy watches her and feels herself unfreeze and flush. She approaches Zoe taking the smallest steps she can, trying to catch her sister's eye. When she hasn't by the time she gets there, Amy whispers: Come with me. But Zoe doesn't answer.

So Amy reaches out and slowly, very slowly, scoops her up and carries her towards the parking lot, across the grass, pausing to point out where the rabbit hutches are. But Zoe doesn't care.

In the car, Zoe starts crying. Their mother opens up the door and bends down to ask Zoe if her sister has said something to upset her. Amy and Zoe both ignore her.

When their mom shuts the door again there is no sound. The only thing there is is Zoe's hands over her seat belt buckle, pulsing. Closer, you can see her tiny fingers twitch.

Now Amy searches Zoe's face. Tears are rolling down it, but Zoe's eyes, always big and brown and sparkly as the campfire, are almost gone. The little slivers of life you can only barely see in the upper right-hand corners tick in place like the stuck hands of a broken watch. But Zoe isn't looking anywhere because her eyes are almost gone.

In a voice more audible than any Amy knew she had, Amy tells her grandfather to drive.

We are going to the doctor now, says Amy, and her words restore the rest of sound.

The engine starts. Their grandma flicks her lighter and sucks smoke into her mouth. The window on her side slides down.

Their grandpa takes one look at Amy in his rearview mirror and takes off.

As the trees and the houses and the streets all slide away from them, Amy searches Zoe's face for Zoe. But Zoe isn't there.

Or where they might be going?

After a while the doctors send them home

They say that sometimes mild concussions lead to episodes like these. She'll be okay, they say. It's nothing to worry about, unless it happens again.

That summer Amy hopes at first to finish her second-grade notebook, but she comes to hate her handwriting, and after a while she gives up. For several weeks in her spare time she reads the books their grandma gives them. She learns that plants eat light, and that the reason we don't all fly into space is gravity. She wants to know why she can't eat light, too, instead of broccoli, which is a plant, and what will happen if the gravity stops working, and what will happen if Zoe gets another mild concussion.

Their grandma says because Amy isn't a plant, and it won't, and she won't.

When a tornado happens at their grandparents' house, day still turns to night and the leaves still get upside down and the cars still disappear, but they also get to hide in the hall closet, which is full of their dad's old games from when he was their age

It is hard to imagine their dad being their age because their dad is gigantic, more than six feet tall, and he has a bunch of gray hair, which their grandparents make all kinds of jokes about when their mom's not there and everyone laughs because they say it must have been because of her his hair went gray. Amy and Zoe are not supposed to tell their mom about these jokes, and they don't.

When they're in the closet at their grandparents', Amy lets them keep the light on even though Zoe is too little for a lot of the games. They play with the dominoes, but Zoe misses the point and knocks them down before it's time to. They play with the marbles, but there's not that much you can do with marbles on a small square of scraggly carpet. If you roll them around they'll just get lost.

Zoe always wants to play Operation, which is where you have to remove the diseases out of Cavity Sam with a pair of tweezers. You have to be really careful because if the tweezers hit the sides of Sam's cavities where his ailments are, his nose lights up, and he buzzes and you lose the game. But Zoe loves the lit-up nose and laughs and laughs, missing the point, asking Amy for permission to mess up one more time.

Their grandparents call it getting sprung when they're let back out of the hall closet, and the reward for getting sprung is pop and cookies. Amy and Zoe are not allowed to drink pop at their house so at their grandparents' they drink all of it they can, and then they jump and jump on the enormous bed upstairs until they're ready for their grandmother to read to them, and then they collapse into all the great big mismatched pillows and spread out like they're making snow angels and follow along in their heads because they always choose the same stories, and they know them all by heart but still get scared each time their grandma switches to her witch's voice, like when Hansel and Gretel get lost. Then the girls straighten up, hands at their hips under the covers, and Zoe scooches over to her sister's side.

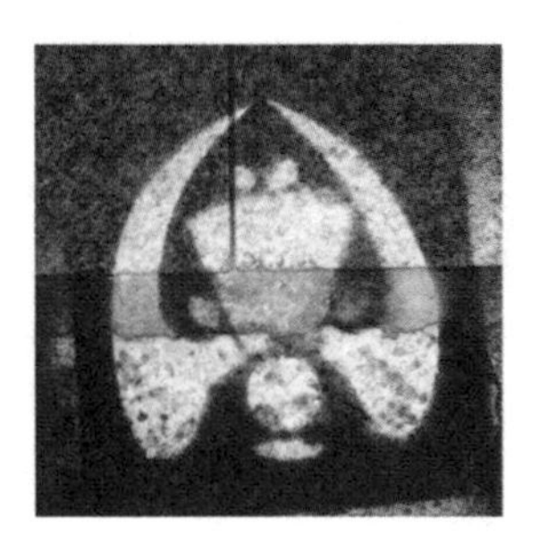

Amy has taken one Polaroid picture of each room at her grandparents' house, including the garage, the backyard, and the front yard, and two of the staircase, since they don't have one at home

One is a close-up of the white metal railing that has a big S with a mustache on its waist between every other bar. The bars look like candy canes that have had their stripes sucked off them and their heads chopped off. The other one shows Zoe sitting sulking on the middle step, overshadowed by the big bright light behind her where the bathroom door opens onto a window that lets in the sun.

In the four years since she's had her camera, Amy's taken fifty-one more pictures of her sister, seven of which feature the dog Santa gave to Zoe last year. The dog is a scruffy Scottish terrier with a black plastic-looking nose. Like Zoe, the dog is wild, and Amy suspects it is a bad influence, eating things off the floor it knows it's not supposed to, like dead bugs and Silly Putty. Amy knows for a fact that Zoe still eats the dog's treats even though she has told her not to more than a million times. But in her camera Amy discovers a way of civilizing both creatures, of teaching them to sit still. They even learn to play dead. Amy takes her pictures carefully because the film is not cheap, making the dog and her sister pose for ages till she gets it just right.

Afterwards the dog trots off to chase some imaginary thing and the girls wait while the picture slowly comes out. Amy lifts it by the tip of the hard white strip at the bottom and waves it gently in the air as the colors begin to bubble out of the shiny gray. Without realizing it the girls both hold their breath.

Every time Zoe asks if she can have the picture, but Amy never says yes. Sometimes Zoe cries, but Amy is never persuaded by tears, and her confidence in her own judgment regarding what is for her sister's own good is total. This way they will have the pictures forever. If she gave them to Zoe now, Zoe would inevitably let the dog have them, and then they would get chewed up and destroyed, like when the birds in the forest eat the path that Hansel made for him and Gretel to go home.

So Amy keeps the pictures inside a secret manila envelope at the bottom of the drawer where she stores the arrowheads and fossils she collects at camp.

Ordinarily the girls only have secrets that they keep together, from their mother.

This is the first secret that exists between them.

Take, for instance, rest, *which used to be the* distance after which a traveler must pause—*which must be what I'm doing now, hopefully maybe finally writing you this letter. (By the way, this picture and its odd word come from a cemetery right here in Berlin.)*

Every summer the girls go to Camp Waluhili with their mom, who works there as a counselor

It's for members of the Camp Fire Girls, which is like Girl Scouts only different. The girls are technically too young to go when they are five and two and six and three and even seven and four, but their mother promises to watch them like a hawk. You have to be careful at camp because it's full of poisonous things: snakes, spiders, scorpions. Some of them can kill you.

The girls always nod when she says this, but they don't really care. Now that they are eight and five they run around and around the meadow until they fall down in the bright yellow flowers and laugh and laugh until they can't breathe.

Amy learns to tie knots, and she is good at it. She learns directions, and she tries to get Zoe to repeat after her: north, east, south, west. You can remember it by saying: never, eat, soggy, waffles, she tells her, but Zoe can't remember all that yet. Amy learns how to build a fire: you put together three pieces of wood in the shape of an A, which is easy to remember, and then you put tinder all along the middle part, but not too much because fires need air. Their mom doesn't let her light the fire, but they sit there with the older girls and eat the s'mores together. Zoe likes to smear the marshmallow on Amy's legs instead of eating it. But then she asks for more.

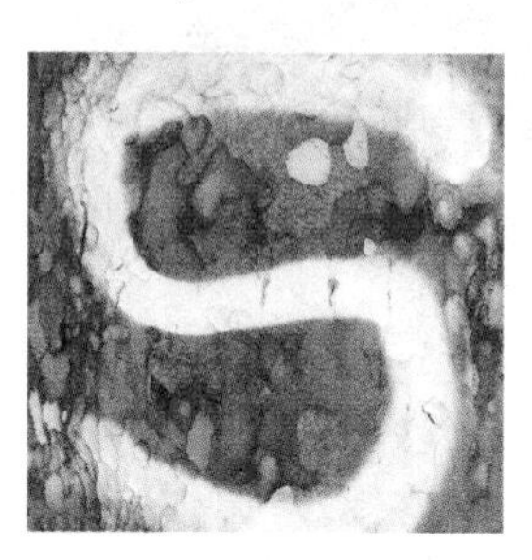

The girls learn to swim. Amy's long body slips into the water like a fish thrown back. But Zoe keeps sinking and getting water in her nose. They give up. They do somersaults in the meadow instead. They play hide and seek. When it takes too long to find Zoe, Amy calls her name, or she says, A to Z, A to Z, over, like it's a Walkie-Talkie, and then she says that it is time to take pictures. Amy takes pictures of Zoe in the trees. She fixes her sister's long light hair that gets tangled when they play. Sometimes she only pretends to take pictures.

In the sun Amy gets freckles, and Zoe turns brown. Together they try and count the freckles on Amy's left arm: twenty-seven, or twenty-eight, or twenty-nine, because they always lose count. The right arm is impossible. Amy and Zoe examine their elbows. They ask their mom what elbows are for. Their mom says to bend their arms. The girls try to do cartwheels in the meadow, but they can't because of their elbows. Zoe tries harder than Amy.

Amy has Zoe help her look for arrowheads and fossils. Zoe finds plain rocks and brings them to Amy to ask if they are fossils. Amy knows all about the Cretaceous period and that we don't know what color the dinosaurs were so they could have been all the colors, even pink, even hot pink. Hot pink is Amy's favorite color, although she pretends it is blue. Amy's favorite dinosaur is the brontosaurus. Amy explains to Zoe that arrowheads were what the Indians used to catch food back when Indians used to live at Waluhili, too. Every summer they find at least one arrowhead, but it takes a lot of work, because arrowheads are little, and you have to look hard between the grass and underneath the dirt.

The fossils are seashells because in the old days all of this was underwater. Sometimes there are fossils with the imprints of different sea plants. The seashells look just like what seashells look like today. They know because their grandmother collects them.

Their mother takes them fishing. There are many words that don't mean what they mean, however, like when their mother cleans the fish they catch. Amy boycotts the results, refusing to eat anything but s'mores those nights, threatening to run away if forced. Zoe does what Amy does and takes the opportunity to eat more s'mores.

Sometimes the girls play games with the campers like Red Rover and tug of war. The older girls like to have Amy on their tug of war team because Amy never lets go. Even if she ends up getting dragged through the mud. Zoe is better at Red Rover because it is easier for her to go berserk, become a human missile, and being so little still, she can often take them by surprise and break right through.

Amy is allowed to learn archery. Zoe complains until something comes along to distract her. The camp teems with butterflies, birds. The older girls stay up late telling ghost stories, but Amy covers her head with a pillow because she likes to wake up when the birds wake up. Sometimes you can spot a bluebird if you're out early, or even a tanager.

Amy takes a picture of the little red suitcase Zoe uses to run away from home

Zoe runs away from home once or twice a week. She takes the dog and goes and sits beneath the pear tree that every year at the tail end of summer produces inedible pears that their dad picks up and throws away. The pear tree is in between the front yard and the backyard, a no man's land, where Zoe believes that no one will think to look for her.

She whiles away the fifteen to twenty minutes it always takes her to run away from home playing with the plastic animal figurines she has packed and distributing provisions evenly between her and the dog. To the dog she gives the brown treats, which are flavored like lamb and vegetable. For herself she reserves the green treats, which are chicken. The peanut butters they share.

On the side of the suitcase containing the figurines and the Milk-Bones is a little drawing of a girl in front of a white picket fence. Above her float the words Going to Grandma's.

But the picture Amy takes does not show this, because what interests Amy is the things the suitcase contains. So while Zoe is in the bathroom Amy snaps it open and lays it splayed atop their rumpled constellation-print sheets. She points her Polaroid down but can't fit it, so she gets on the bed and stands over it, points, and pulls the shutter swiftly with her forefinger.

Of the numerous plastic animal figurines in her collection, Zoe has chosen one elephant and a family of giraffes. Then, in addition to the small box of Milk-Bones, there is a toothbrush, one sock with a friendly-looking shark that prowls the ankle, and a framed five-by-seven photograph, black and white, of Dorothy holding Toto up to her cheek, the two of them gazing off into the distance. The photograph takes up a massive percentage of the space inside the little red suitcase, and Amy wonders why her sister takes it when she runs away from home, since it is just a piece of someone else's junk they got at a garage sale.

Then Zoe comes back from the bathroom and catches Amy red-handed, still standing over her stuff, and she screams and hollers like a wild banshee until Amy offers her a piece of tropical fruit punch gum.

Or dwell, *which used to mean* to lead astray.
(I took this picture right around the corner from where we used to live, in Paris.)

Amy takes pictures of everywhere they go

They go to Lincoln, Nebraska, for their family vacation, and Amy takes pictures of the dinosaurs at the Museum of Natural History. Zoe always wants to be in the pictures, and usually Amy says yes, but on occasion, Amy says no. Then Zoe cries until someone else takes her picture in the same spot. Amy on the other hand does not like to have her picture taken and rarely smiles when she is urged to pose.

Amy likes the dinosaurs but not the stuffed owls, which she says are disgusting because they are dead. Amy knows the dinosaurs are dead, too, but it's different because they're almost more like rocks. Zoe makes a face when Amy says the word dead or the word disgusting. She sticks her tongue out and scrunches up her little nose.

Their other grandparents live in Kansas in between Oklahoma and Nebraska, but their mom says she does not want to visit them on the way back because they're assholes. Their dad says not to say bad words in front of the girls.

They go to the Porter Peach Festival in Porter, Oklahoma, and Amy takes pictures of peaches until the dog runs away, and they all have to chase it. But when they've caught it, they all get to eat fresh peaches with vanilla ice cream. Even the dog eats peaches. They are all sweaty and smelly and filled up with sugar. Amy and Zoe and their mother sing camp songs the whole way home until their dad turns on the radio.

At the Tulsa State Fair Amy takes pictures of the roller coaster and the stands selling corn dogs and cotton candy and of Zoe with cotton candy like spiderwebs in her hair. Zoe cries until their dad buys her some more cotton candy to eat. At the Fair there is a petting zoo where the girls get to feed farm animals, but their mom has to take away the food sometimes because Zoe likes to try the little pellets of alfalfa herself. At these confiscations, Amy howls with laughter, and Zoe's eyes get wide.

At the real zoo Amy learns to stand like a flamingo, one foot in the crook of the other leg's knee, and she can stand this way in silence just observing the birds for as long as it takes Zoe to run around the prairie dogs a dozen times.

They ride their bikes in the parking lot at the Tulsa Teachers Credit Union three doors down from their house when it's not business hours and their dad can take them. Their dad still rides his old green Schwinn with the baby seat on the back even though neither one of them is a baby anymore, and he calls it Gone with the Schwinn to their mom whenever they are heading out. Then they have races around the big post in the middle of the parking lot and from the dumpster to the main doors. You have to get up onto the sidewalk to win.

Lately Zoe keeps talking about getting her training wheels off although Amy keeps reminding her that even with them on she always manages to find a way to topple over, and if she hadn't had her helmet on she could have killed herself a thousand times or gotten another concussion, and besides, Zoe is only five and a quarter, and Amy is almost eight and a half and just got hers off last year. But Zoe doesn't care and keeps on talking about it.

Amy always has to remind Zoe repeatedly about everything. Like to drink the rest of her juice and to keep her shoes on and not to water the bonsai in their room so it will not drown like the last one. It is exhausting taking care of young children. Usually their mom and dad are too distracted so Amy does it, even though it leaves her barely any time.

They go to Tahlequah for the Intertribal Powwow, and Amy takes pictures of real teepees, tall as the sky. The Indians wear leather dresses with leather strings and turquoise beads and feathers and circles that symbolize things. The Indian children get to wear feathers, too. The Cherokees have lots of different symbols to mean different things. Amy wants to learn them all. She begins to invent new symbols for her and Zoe only, so they can write notes to each other without their mother interfering.

Their mother has told them that once one of the other counselors at Camp Waluhili got bitten by a black widow, and the venom spread so fast they had to cut out part of her leg. So she had a hole in her leg, and she kept secret things inside it, like messages. Now Amy twists this story around. To send and receive secret messages you don't need to be poisoned or have any particular place. What you need is a secret system, a network of secret shapes.

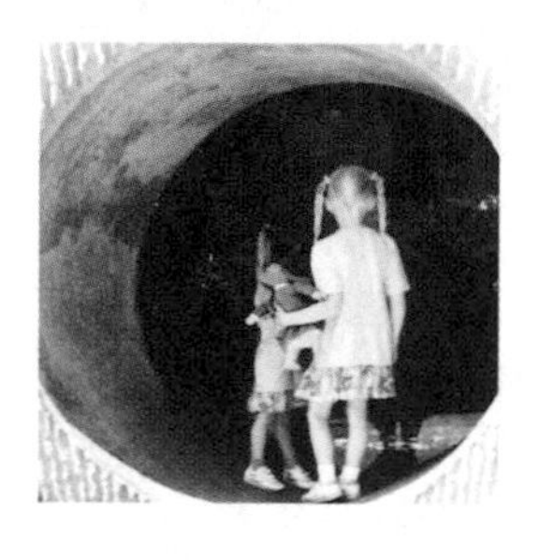

So she makes Zoe practice drawing the symbols for dog and home and mom and dad and grandparents and hungry and thirsty and Cruella de Vil and Garfield and Raggedy Ann and Raggedy Andy and Target and radio. The symbol for dinosaurs is a dinosaur because Amy can't think of anything better. Zoe practices diligently at first and then goes off to play with the dog, leaving sloppy scrawlings all over the floor that Amy picks up, emitting a slow sigh she has learned from their grandmother, the gradual deflation of a balloon.

Even the simplest words keep secrets. The more you take a word for granted, the less it tells.

The night before the girls go back to school their mom tells them what sex is and reads them a story about a woman in a car crash off a bridge

Good Housekeeping says if you crash your car off a bridge you should rescue your husband from drowning if you can, because if you have a husband you can make more children, whereas if you rescue your child you'll only ever have that one. Their mom thinks about that a lot. What she would do if they got into a car crash off a bridge. The girls begin to practice how long they can hold their breath when they are alone in their room.

The girls dance and dance and dance to Paul Simon's Graceland in the dining room, working themselves up into a frenzy, while their mom makes oatmeal fudgies in the kitchen for them to take for Labor Day to school

Then Zoe, wanting to hear I Know What I Know again, goes and plucks the needle off the record, resulting in a scratch. Amy leaps in and snatches the record away. A scuffle ensues. Zoe bursts into tears. Amy lets the record droop down a little in her hands. Zoe sniffs, purses her lips, and looks back and forth between Graceland and her sister's face.

Then she lunges forward and pries at the record with all her might until it snaps in half.

In the stunned silence that follows this, before their mother comes in and screams at them that this was a library record and that now they'll have to pay and go to your room, Zoe looks at Amy, and Amy looks directly ahead, at the two rows of four plates that hang from the white wall. Each plate features a ghost ship, which their mom has explained is when a ship sinks and all its traces disappear into the sea. And it's like people who die but don't get buried: the ships turn into ghosts. Sailors see them floating out on the water, aflame. Of the eight plates six of them are half obscured by bright orange fire.

If Amy could go back a few seconds, she would break the plates with her sister, one by one, rather than the record, which was something they loved and now will never have again.

In ancient Greece a scruple *was a* pebble stuck inside your shoe.

Amy is the tallest kid in her grade, and the fastest, and the best at math

She comes first during roll call and gets only straight A's. Their school uses a Japanese kind of math called Kumon that lets you do however many problems you want in an hour. Amy likes to do a lot of problems without making mistakes. All the other kids disappear when she starts doing her Kumon. All she is aware of is those numbers. She loves numbers and letters and practices to improve her handwriting every evening at home.

One day in the middle of long division a hand reaches inside her bubble and attaches itself to hers. Amy gasps without meaning to. She looks up and sees the principal.

Most children dread the appearance of the school principal at their desk, but Amy is so well behaved that it does not occur to her to worry. When the principal asks her to come outside with her please, Amy politely declines. But then when she sees the stunned scandalized eyes of the principal she sets her pencil down.

In the back of the ambulance, her sister has been taken over by a ghost

Their mom gets as strong as a superhero and holds her down. Amy and Zoe had always assumed it would be fun to ride in an ambulance or a fire truck or a police car because you would get to go fast and break all the rules and not stop at any lights. But now Zoe isn't Zoe, and everything is wrong. Zoe throws up but doesn't know she's throwing up, so the throw-up just drips down her chin and onto the lavender-colored dress that used to be Amy's favorite, and the lady who works for the ambulance mops it off her, but Amy fears the towel will scratch her sister's face.

Unlike the last time, Zoe's eyes are white, as though she's been erased. Her whole body jerks to one side at a rhythm that is not a human rhythm. Amy screams, Zoe, Zoe, Zoe, but Zoe isn't there. Their mom gets angry and says to shut up because she's making everything worse. Then every fiber of Amy's body screams, in silence. Zoe, Zoe, Zoe.

Oh Zoe.

The ambulance takes them to the pink hospital by their grandparents' house

Amy recognizes it when they all pile out. This isn't where they went the last time, and this time Zoe and their mom run away into a secret room where the nurses won't let Amy go. Amy is told to sit and wait.

Amy sits and waits. She tastes like salt, and the wet neck of her T-shirt sticks to her skin. She squeezes and unsqueezes her hands in her lap. She looks around and sees the room is full of dirty people yellowed by the light, not sitting up straight. She would like to go look for her sister, but she is scared that if she doesn't sit and wait they'll never let her see her sister again. She looks down at her hands, whitened at the knuckles, splashed. The old man sitting across from her begins to cry, and Amy's own eyes dry up, and she would like to hold the old man's hand, but she is scared he might have germs and scared that if she doesn't sit and wait she'll get in trouble, and then they'll never let her see her sister again.

Oh Zoe, what does it mean to have already
done something you know you'd never do?

Amy knows exactly what she would do if they got into a car crash off a bridge

She would unbuckle her sister's seat belt and then unbuckle hers as she was simultaneously rolling down the window on her side of the car. Then they would swim out the window holding hands until they got to the top of the river. If it is winter Amy knows for a fact that she can simply kick through the ice because there is never all that much in the middle of the river, only around the edges.

Sometimes their mom sings them lullabies, and Amy likes her voice but not the songs

Zoe doesn't listen to the words, but Amy does. Zoe always asks for the one about the boat, which goes like this:

> O there was a lofty ship and she sailed upon the sea
> And the name of the ship was the Golden Vanity
> And she feared she would be taken by the Turkish enemy
> As she sailed upon the lowland, low low lowland,
> Sailed upon the lowland sea.
>
> Now up stepped a cabin boy, a cabin boy was he,
> And he said to the captain, What will you give to me
> If I sneak along the side of the Turkish enemy
> And I sink her in the lowland, low low lowland,
> Sink her in the lowland sea.
>
> O I will give you silver, and I will give you gold
> And the hand of my daughter if you will be so bold
> As to swim along the side of the Turkish enemy
> And to sink her in the lowland, low low lowland,
> Sink her in the lowland sea.
>
> Well, up jumped the cabin boy, and overboard went he
> And he swam along the side of the Turkish enemy,
> And with brace and a bit he bore holes one, two, and three,
> And he sank her in the lowland, low low lowland,
> Sank her in the lowland sea.

Then he swam to the side of the Golden Vanity,
And he called to the captain to pull him from the sea
But the captain would not heed, for his daughter he did need,
So they left him in the lowland, low low lowland,
Left him in the lowland sea.

Then his mates pulled him up, and on the deck he died,
And they wrapped him in a sail, so very square and wide,
And they threw him overboard to float out upon the tide,
But he sank beneath the lowland, low low lowland,
Sank beneath the lowland sea.

By the last verse Amy's stomach churns, causing her to writhe beneath their puppy-print sheets and their mother's mother's scratchy, bulky quilt, although nobody can tell.

It's so hard for me now to understand myself then, which makes me want to trace things back to where they started, and sometimes I wonder if it might have been that afternoon I burned my black dress in the sink.

Nobody can tell what's really wrong with Zoe, not even the doctors, not for a long time

Their mom says that's because the doctors don't know what they are doing, but their dad says, Leslie, like it might be their mom who doesn't know.

They do different tests like the one where she has to go inside a tunnel and lie still so they can take pictures of her brain. Amy learns the difference between an MRI and a CAT scan. She knows MRIs are more expensive but that they need to do them anyway. She knows there are magnets inside the tunnel that are very strong because you have to take off your earrings before you go into the room.

At first they don't let Amy go in. At first she has to wait outside with their dad. She tries to practice her handwriting, but now the lead in her pencil always breaks.

But Zoe won't lie still. At first they give her shots to make her, but Zoe is so scared of the shots that she begs and begs and begs until the nurses take the needles back. Then Amy starts to be the one to sit in the room with her sister. Amy knows the knock-knock jokes to tell, like the lettuce in, we're freezing, and the orange you glad I didn't say banana.

Amy stops taking pictures except of Zoe's dog, to bring to Zoe when she has to have her blood taken, because they don't let dogs in hospitals. There is nothing in the world worse than Zoe having her blood taken. Amy tries to show her the pictures at just the right moment, just right before the nurse puts the needle in, between when they put the gray tie around her arm and when they put the needle in.

Amy believes that if she can get the timing exactly right, Zoe will forget about what's happening.

But Amy can't get the timing exactly right. She is always too early or too late. Zoe still sobs and begs the nurses not to hurt her.

Zoe's arms are bruised all over from all the times they have to take her blood. Amy doesn't look at the bags as they fill up because if she does she starts to feel funny like she's floating and like she might fall down. But she knows she can't fall down because what would Zoe do.

Zoe has more seizures, and now they just drive to the hospital because ambulances cost a lot of money. Amy sits in the back seat with her sister and tries to talk herself into believing that her sister's still there.

One day Zoe and the dog are intercepted by the neighbors two doors down

She is returned to their house carrying her little red suitcase in one hand and a Hula-Hoop in the other. She claims upon interrogation to be looking for the circus. She holds out the Hula-Hoop an inch or so off the ground and encourages the dog to come through it. The dog sits and blinks a couple of quick blinks, and Amy laughs, and Zoe bursts into tears.

I'd seen it in a movie once, and when we got home from the funeral, it seemed like the right thing to do, but I didn't think about the smoke, which scared you, or how mad Mom and Dad would be when they came back because the dress was new, and I was putting you in danger.

Zoe starts taking medication that makes her wet the bed

The warmth of her urine wakes Amy up. She gets up and goes to their parents' room and shakes their mom by the shoulder to come and change the sheets. Their mom comes and picks Zoe up and carries her into their room, placing her on her side of their bed. Zoe does not wake up. Sometimes their dad wakes up, and sometimes he doesn't, because a lot of times he's tired from his commute.

Finally the doctors find the tumor. The tumor is located in the left frontal lobe. The tumor is called a pilocytic astrocytoma. It is rare but the good news is it's benign which means it doesn't spread. Amy practices spelling pilocytic astrocytoma out loud like you do in spelling bees. Everyone is impressed that she can spell such long words. She can also spell benign even though it sounds like be nine, which Amy thinks is funny because she is about to be nine at the end of September, like the word is a message for her.

One day their parents decide to do surgery in spite of the risks. Later, when Zoe is asleep, Amy asks their mom what are the risks. Their mom says that the brain is very sensitive, and that if you operate on it, you run the risk of altering it. You can in fact completely change a person's personality, because the brain controls everything, and for example there have been people who have had accidents that have affected their brains, and then they become criminals, or they just can't think anymore.

Now Amy doesn't sleep. It doesn't wake her up when her sister wets the bed because she doesn't sleep. Their dad buys an aquarium to put in their room because he says the fish are soothing. The aquarium has different kinds of fish in it: angelfish, minnows, and a little catfish that lives at the bottom where the rocks are.

Amy lies awake and looks at the fish. One by one the catfish eats the minnows by pulling them apart.

Amy is relieved when Zoe wets the bed so she can go and get their parents. But then everyone falls asleep again, leaving her alone.

Once there was a boy at camp who loved fish

Boys are not allowed at their camp, but this boy was somebody's younger brother, and for some reason, he got special permission. He would follow their mom around all day whenever she would let him because he fell a little bit in love with her, even though he must have only been eleven or twelve. This was all a long time ago, before Amy and Zoe were born.

The boy was always talking about his aquarium at home and all the exotic fish he had. He always did his homework fast so he could take care of his fish. He cleaned the tank a lot and watched them and played them different kinds of music.

One day when he became a teenager he committed suicide. Their mom says it proves he didn't know what he was doing that he shot himself in front of the aquarium, breaking the glass, and spilling all the fish out. Their mom says he didn't die right away. His parents came running into the room when they heard the gunshot and found him lying on the floor in salt water, blood, flopping fish, and broken glass. He was saying, Shit, shit, shit, like that, over and over, and then he died.

Their dad doesn't like for their mom to say bad words to them because he says they're too young, but their mom says that's just the way the world is, she didn't make the words up.

She says suicide is the most selfish thing you can do, and to never do it.

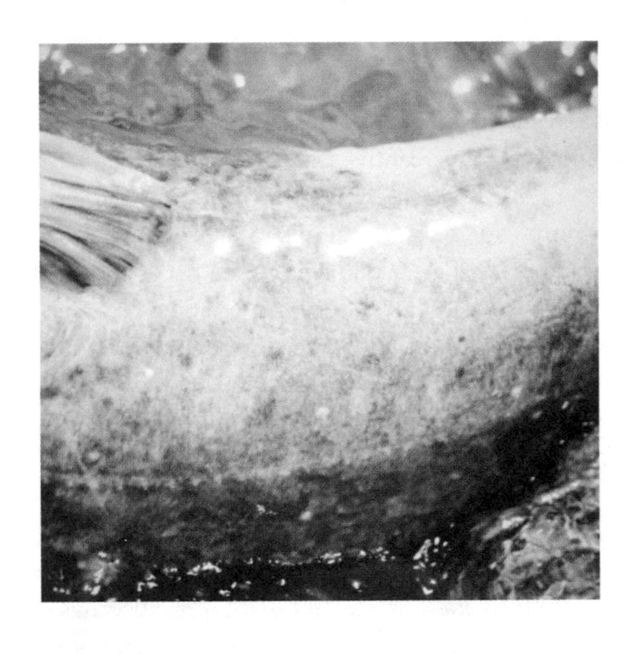

Do you ever get our memories mixed up, Zoe?

Sometimes when they all go to the hospital together, their dad takes Amy to the maternity ward to see the babies

Amy loves to look at the babies. Amy is tall for her age, in the ninety-ninth percentile, and can, when she stands on tiptoes, peer inside the big window that shows the cradles all lined up with the babies asleep in them. Amy knows that babies sleep a lot. Their dad says when her sister was born Amy wanted to hold her all the time, but sometimes their mom had to hold her, to feed her, and then Amy would get angry and stomp around and throw tantrums. This makes Amy smile because she knows she ended up with Zoe as hers anyway.

Amy doesn't like the food at the hospital cafeteria, which is mushy and cold. Most of the people sitting in the cafeteria are either doctors or nurses or sad. Sometimes their parents make Amy stay there for long stretches coloring in her coloring book or practicing her secret alphabet, writing notes to Zoe. Sometimes she has to wait outside her sister's room in the pediatric ward with the children who are terminal. What terminal means is going to die, but their dad says not all of them are, but then their mom says, Rick, what's the point, which Amy takes to mean they are because their dad just looks down at his big old boots and doesn't answer.

No matter how hard she tries to only look at her notebook, the dying children's parents always start to talk with Amy. Sometimes she's even doing Kumon. But the parents of the dying children interrupt her and tell her she looks just like a little doll. Everyone says the same thing, that she looks like a doll. Amy feels funny when they say it, a little sick to her stomach. She doesn't really know what they mean. Why would she look like a doll when she's a person? Or do they just mean she doesn't have any scratches on her skin like the dying kids do? She doesn't ask their mom because their mom seems annoyed when people say it when she's there. From this she deduces that she is right to feel uncomfortable.

Their mom takes her to see the babies and tells her about when she was born. Amy was born early because their mom stepped on a snake in the garage and got scared, and that induced the labor. Because of the snake Amy had to stay in the hospital a little bit longer, in a cradle just like these ones. Amy asks if the snake got away, hoping the answer is yes. The answer is no.

Amy, liberated by a snake that died, feels guilty and important. Their mom takes her to the cafeteria for lunch but gets mad at her in the middle and goes back down to the pediatric ward without her. She doesn't give Amy any instructions on what to do next, so Amy decides to find the maternity ward by herself. She remembers never eat soggy waffles, and anyway, she remembers where it is. She stands at the window for a long time, watching the babies sleep. She fogs the glass up with her breath. She draws a tiny heart in the mist with her fingertip, and she loves the squeaking sound this makes, so she moves a little to the left and fogs up the glass again, on purpose, and draws a slightly bigger heart.

Then she gets in trouble for disappearing, but it is worth it.

At home Amy takes her pictures out of her fossil drawer and goes over them one by one, looking for clues about the tumor

She begins at the beginning. The first picture she has is from Christmas Day of the five-foot polyester teepee set up in the living room next to the tree. Every Christmas Eve the girls get to spend the night inside the teepee while Santa and his reindeer go around the world. Their aim is always to stay up all night, and officially it is the one night of the year when even their mom says they have no bedtime.

And at first, in the gentle glow of the thousand tiny lights strung around and around the tree, diffuse through the teepee's tan fabric, Amy sees her sister's enormous brown eyes gleam. As long as Amy permits it Zoe recites her Christmas list: a puppy, a dollhouse, a tree house, a trampoline, a puppy, new crayons, some new movies, a leash with sparkles and colors on it, puppy stickers, a water gun, a princess crown, a book about puppies.

You can't read Zoe's handwriting yet, and Zoe can't spell, so Amy is the one to make the lists. Zoe insists on putting puppy twice so Santa knows it's important.

And in fact at the moment this first picture is taken Zoe is in the study, still by the fireplace squeezing her little Scottish terrier to her face.

By the time the reindeer land on top of their house and Santa comes down and eats the cookies and drinks the milk they set out for him on the mantel, the girls have always fallen asleep. Zoe falls first after a prolonged struggle. Amy pretends to fall asleep first, but secretly she watches over her sister's hot little body curled up against her, breath quick, feet shuffling, a tight, pulsing ball of pure desire. Then slowly Zoe succumbs, and Amy lets herself follow.

As if by magic the teepee always fits them, even though they grow.

Amy holds the picture out by the tip of the hard white strip at the bottom and brings it back up to her face, scrutinizing and recalling. She weighs in her mind her sister's heartbeat versus the jerks and twitches of her body during seizures, looks to see if she can see.

It seems impossible that Zoe got a tumor while Amy did not. The girls almost always get sick at the same time: chicken pox, strep throat, colds. Then it's fun because their dad reads them stories like the one about the duck that turns into a swan and their mom brings them glasses of Tang. Unless Amy does have a brain tumor but no one knows yet. In that case her personality might already be changing. In that case she might already be becoming a completely different person, but nobody has noticed, and Amy can't notice because it's her brain that's getting switched.

Amy slips the teepee picture back into the envelope. She examines all the pictures of their house, searching for the culprit: the pantry with the light switched on, the kitchen, the dining room looking towards the living room so you don't see those plates with the shipwrecks and the boys that drown, the long oak church pew in the living room where no one ever sits, the smooth cool concrete of the front porch, the giant tree in the backyard with the sun behind it, their dad's study that takes up almost a third of the whole house, the very long driveway and clear down at the end of it the garage like a little separate house with the basketball goal affixed to its peeling white siding, the coats in the entryway, their room with its invisible line drawn down the middle separating order from chaos, their mom's desk in the hallway between their parents' room and their room, their parents' room, the bathroom with the bathtub bubbly before their mom gets in.

She looks and looks like the doctors do at CAT scans, but she keeps on not seeing it, even though she knows it must be there.

Because for me they bleed over sometimes, like when I think of your first ambulance and see my own body instead, thudding down an endless sidewalk on a stretcher clutching what's left of my stuffed octopus as frat boys spill out of their houses and line up to watch.

Amy and Zoe are taking time off school

This is because Zoe can't go to school anymore because she has to have surgery, and surgery is expensive, so Amy can't go either, because they can't afford to pay. Their mom says the public schools won't let Amy do her Kumon, and they'll make her do everything at grade level like addition and subtraction. This makes Amy laugh because she finished addition and subtraction a long time ago, but then she sees their mom seems serious and tries to correct her face.

The girls watch a lot of TV now, not only the cartoons on Saturday mornings. Sometimes Amy reads out loud to Zoe. Zoe likes Dr. Seuss books, and Amy does different voices for different characters. She practices at night in the bathroom so she doesn't get tripped up on the rhymes. Zoe's favorite is The Cat in the Hat. Amy's favorite is Horton Hears a Who!, but Zoe says she doesn't like that one because it's boring. Amy says she doesn't like The Cat in the Hat because it's stupid, although she reads it to Zoe anyway.

Eventually they compromise on Green Eggs and Ham. Gradually Amy teaches Zoe to read it herself.

Amy and Zoe both know that the surgery is coming up soon. But they watch TV and read their Dr. Seuss books and ride their bikes with their dad. Amy makes Zoe keep practicing their address. Zoe laughs when she remembers and cries when she can't. Zoe never knows the zip code.

Their parents tell Zoe that she can have any present she wants after her surgery in exchange for being brave. For several days the girls make lists. Zoe paces up and down their bedroom like she might explode. Finally she decides on a pair of cowgirl boots. Amy says she should ask for something better than cowgirl boots, like moccasins, but there is no reasoning with Zoe, she wants the boots.

A fight breaks out between their parents. Their mom stays at home with Zoe while Amy and their dad go to Drysdales North South East and Western Wear. They look around at the bandannas and silver buckles, and then they choose a pair of little square-toed ropers with yellow tops with stitching in different-colored threads that looks like a cross between a happy cat and a fireplace. Their dad puts his hand on Amy's shoulder and says for the second time that money is no object. She doesn't look at him.

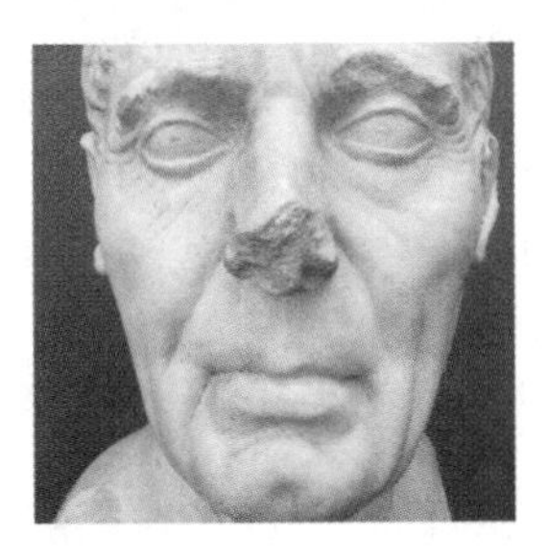

They take the boots to the salesgirl and realize they don't know Zoe's size. Amy hears her dad make a noise. She is trying to calculate what size her sister wears based on her size and how long it usually takes for Zoe to fit into her shoes. Then she realizes that their dad is crying, sitting down on one of the benches for trying things on. She says a size. The salesgirl disappears into the back to find it.

On the day before the surgery they all go to their grandparents' house and have root beer floats and watch TV and Sleeping Beauty

Amy and Zoe huddle very close together as though the air conditioning is making them cold. After the movie's over Zoe and their parents get up and start to walk out to the car. Their grandparents stay where they are, sitting on either side of the entertainment center. Amy sits with them until she hears the car doors. She runs to the shut front door and stands on her tiptoes and watches them through the bottom blue square in the stained-glass window while they pull out of the driveway and into the street, the glass fogging up except where her nose is pressed against it. Slowly her fingertips slide down the slick groove of the wood.

When the phone rings the ground drops out and Zoe is gone

It rings like a drill, insistent. Amy hears their grandma take a drag off her cigarette, and then she picks it up. Amy is lying on the sofa, back to the TV like she is taking a nap, although she isn't sleeping.

A gash opens up in her head, and she brings her hands up to her skull as though to keep it all from falling out.

Their grandpa says not to mess up her pretty hair. Their grandma shushes him. Then she hangs up and comes over and puts her hand on Amy's shoulder. Amy curls up. Their grandma says very quietly in almost a whisper that her sister has just been wheeled into surgery. She does not say that everything will be all right. For one second, Amy reaches around and grasps her grandma's hand. Then she jumps up and runs into the bathroom and vomits. You can't eat anything before surgery, so all she throws up is fluids from her own body, which taste like poison.

To worry *used to mean* to strangle.

While her sister's in the hospital, Amy is in charge of the dog

She tries to teach it different tricks like fetch to surprise Zoe when she gets out, but the dog won't learn.

After a few days, Amy is allowed to visit. She is so scared her sister might have changed personality from the surgery that her hands won't stop shaking on the way. When she walks into the room she sees an alien lying in a little bed with all kinds of different tubes and wires coming out of its body. It takes her a second to understand what is happening. Her sister's long streaked hair is all gone, and all across her bare little skull is a jagged dark red wound. Without wanting to Amy bursts into tears. Her hands fly to her face to cover it up, but it is too late because their mother is already angry. Before she is dragged back out of the room she gets a look at her sister's eyes. They are dull, and hollow.

Amy lies on her grandparents' couch all day with her face in the cushion, curled up like a seashell.

One day at the hospital Amy tries to play Chutes and Ladders with some dying kids, but after just a little while they say she's cheating, and she has to go back to just waiting

She knows it's not her fault she's lucky, but it makes her stomach hurt. Her head gets so bad she can't see straight. She tries to lie down on the floor with her eyes closed, but she gets caught.

The journeys a word makes are not fully fathomable (a fathom *was once an* embrace, *or the measure of an armspan), part of what sets it apart from its semantic kin, giving rise to words that look the same and come from the same home but that mean completely different things now, like* casualty *and* casualidad *(which is just* coincidence *in Spanish).*

Zoe is released from the hospital on Amy's tenth birthday

It is September 24, 1991. Amy's party, held at their grandparents' house, is attended by all the relatives and extended relatives from all over Oklahoma. Even their cousins who live in Oklahoma City come. At first Amy and Zoe hold hands because Zoe is very weak and not used to walking, but then people come and crowd around Zoe, and Amy is jostled away. Gradually Amy drifts over to the doorway and keeps an eye on Zoe, silent.

Now when they go anywhere everyone stares at Zoe. They try putting different types of hats on her, but she hates them all. She insists on wearing her cowgirl boots regardless of whether or not they are appropriate. They are slightly too big for her, but if she wears two or three pairs of socks, they are fine.

Sometimes now the girls go and hide in the hall closet not because there might be a tornado but just because. Their parents say that they will homeschool them from now on because their dad is a college teacher anyway, and their mom knows a lot about a lot of things because she was the salutatorian of her high school class and would have been the valedictorian except for one of her teachers who was a jerk, so it will actually be better than school. This is fine with them. The only people they want to see are each other anyway.

Amy starts taking pictures again, but only occasionally, and almost always of Zoe.

When they go in for Zoe's checkups they get to go to LaFortune Park afterwards and look at the ducks. One time they see one of the ducklings get snapped up by a snapping turtle, leaving only bubbles on the surface of the pond. They stand there looking for a little while, finding it hard to believe. Their mom says that's the way the world works, but they don't care: they don't want to go anymore. So then their mom says fine, pretend, and they go straight to their grandparents' house after checkups instead. Amy sits very quiet beside her sister almost like she is her sister and her own body's just an empty ghost.

A lot of times their grandparents play Scrabble while they watch TV. Their grandparents always get into arguments over whether words are words or not, but their grandma is always the scorekeeper, so she always wins. They argue fondly, and the girls enjoy it, although their grandpa claims that sometimes their grandma stabs him with her pencil, and he does have big blue marks on the backs of his hands, but they have never seen her do it in all their time there, so they're not sure. Their grandpa also told them one time when they went to Camp Waluhili that he would fax them some cookies, but then they found out you couldn't fax cookies, and they began to view him as a jokester, an unreliable source.

Amy takes a picture of Zoe on the couch with the dog and the octopus with big huge eyes

The octopus is a gift from their grandparents for Amy's birthday. They each got one. It's the size of a baby but with eight purple arms. For the picture Zoe sets it on top of the dog's head like a funny hat. She is blurred because she is laughing, but you can still make out the dimples in her cheeks, and in back of them the hollows.

Words owe their very existence to distance,
although their deepest purpose is to overcome it;
this is the truest in instances like homesick, *a*
word I've always loved—but never thought I'd
feel, until today.

For Christmas they get matching pairs of tennis shoes from their grandparents

The shoes are the same dark orange as their mom's car only with black zigzag stripes. They have Velcro instead of laces because Zoe hasn't learned to tie her shoes yet. The best thing about them is they have tiger paws on the soles, which means the girls get to leave paw prints wherever they go. They intentionally track mud into the kitchen even though they know they'll get in trouble. Zoe forgets about her cowgirl boots, except when they dress up to go to church.

In the backyard they play with the roly-polies that live at the trunk of the tree. The roly-polies bustle around like quicker caterpillars, but when you pick them up and hold them gently between your fingers they turn into hard little gray balls. The girls collect them in a bucket and then let them loose.

They no longer take their baths together because Amy doesn't want to. Zoe's tantrums only result in a reduction in bath times for everyone because their mom says it's just not worth it.

Their dad loses his job and at first the girls are thrilled. Their mom goes and works in an office, and the girls spend days on end poring over their dad's atlas sitting on either side of him, asking questions over every picture on every page. They learn all the animals on Madagascar and make mazes they refer to as Black Forests, with coded maps that Amy hides around the house for Zoe. Their dad lets them use his big old T-shirts as saris. They check out cassette tapes from the library with Japanese flute music and salsa from a forbidden island kingdom the girls assume has treasure in the coves. Zoe points out that no one's proven there aren't fairies living there. They would likely fit inside your pocket and you'd just have to be careful not to squish them when you're sitting down, but otherwise they'd take you to the treasure probably. Amy informs Zoe that fairies don't exist. But she says what there could be is species considered erroneously by the scientists to be extinct.

Then their dad starts interfering in things and covering Zoe's eyes when kissing comes on TV or when one person shoots another person and there's blood. It used to be they could do whatever they wanted because their mom was always reading mystery novels in the other room. Now Amy runs out of time for Kumon, and Zoe runs out of time for her plastic animals. The girls confer and adopt a strategy that consists in pretending they want to take a nap in the middle of the school day, which allows them at least a couple of hours of freedom in their room. Amy's pretty tired of sharing, but she's been told repeatedly there is no way for each of them to have a room. Amy explains to Zoe how when she grows up her room will have the make-believe grass they use on football fields and walls the color of the sky, with clouds, but Zoe says she doesn't want her own room and gets a look on her face like she's about to cry.

After naptime he takes them on bike rides or drags them to the racetrack to teach them about luck, which he calls probability. They start going to the mall to ask the salesgirls if they can have a free sample of perfume. Whatever they get Zoe uses up her share of in a day, spraying herself in the face every few minutes until she stinks. Amy holds the tiny vials up to the ceiling light and peers inside. Then she tucks them away inside the shoebox in her fossil drawer like relics.

Sometimes they go to the MedEx around the corner from the Tulsa Teachers Credit Union to look around. Zoe wants everything, and sometimes their dad says she can have anything she wants that costs less than a dollar. One day she gets a bone for the dog. One day she gets a barrette. Her hair is starting to grow back now, although it isn't long enough yet for a barrette. As it grows it gets darker and darker, and one day their grandma says they don't even look like sisters anymore, what with Amy being so fair-haired, like before. So Amy tries wearing her sister's hats, but she finds they give her headaches.

The next Christmas the girls discover they no longer fit into the teepee. They ask for a new teepee knowing they are asking for something impossible. They build themselves a fort in the living room out of chairs from the dining room and out-of-season sheets, and afterwards they stand together in the entryway surveying their creation. That night they stay up all night talking in their fort, and the next day after stockings they nap all morning in the soft light of the Christmas tree filtered through the lake-colored cotton.

The girls like to dance together when their parents aren't home

Their mom still works half-time but now with meetings in the afternoons and sometimes little trips to places like Owasso, and their dad has started taking teaching gigs. One day the girls see an ice-skating routine on TV set to swing dance music, and the next time they know it's going to be on they tape it so they can watch it again and practice. Zoe likes the part where Amy picks her up and swings her around. Zoe picks the dog up and swings it around, too.

The ice skaters they like all come from the former Soviet Union. In Europe the countries can change sometimes depending on the politics—they already know this from their dad. Now the girls learn that some of the people from the former Soviet Union use a different kind of alphabet, and they ask their mom to take them to the library so they can learn it. They find out that the Russian alphabet has five letters more than the English alphabet. Amy practices writing out the new shapes. Amy, having invented numerous alphabets that her sister has consistently failed to learn, thereby precluding the exchange of private communications, now gets hopeful that a real foreign language may turn out to be the way to go.

The only downside is the Soviets have jumbled up their many letters, and Z is in the middle, not at the end. Alphabetical order has always been Amy's favorite, better than chronological and a vast improvement over order of importance. Zoe, on the other hand, has long complained at the injustice of an alphabet that always puts her last. She considers this new system at least a partial vengeance of the Z's upon the A's: now Z is seventh, as though it's catching up.

Zoe wants to learn a language, too, but isn't sure if what she wants to learn is Russian because by now the girls have learned that Zoe's favorite ice skaters are from Ukraine which has recently turned into a separate place from Russia.

Their parents are astonished to discover a true feud arising between their daughters; more astonishing still is that the source of the feud is a question of sovereignty in Eastern Europe. The girls build separate forts in the living room now with their octopi posted as sentries at the entry flaps and reproductions in crayon of their respective nations' flags, Russia meticulous red and navy stripes, Ukraine some yellow ovals floating over light blue zigzags.

Although their father is a geographer, no one in the family has a passport; it has never occurred to anyone to learn another language. But their parents are pleased to find them motivated to learn, and so they try to broker a truce between them by finding someone who can tutor them in both languages.

This only intensifies the fighting.

Some words surface in proximity, like swimmers moving in the same direction, keeping the same pace, who nonetheless have never met and never will—like Russian's гриф, *which means* vulture, *although it is pronounced like* grief; *the same thing happens to people on trains and buses, and pedestrians.*

Overlaps like these need not be meaningless,
although they happen for no reason—even mean
has also meant to hold in common, to remember,
to long for, *and* to love.

Amy and Zoe fall in love for the first time, at the same time, with the same boy

Sasha is a former student of their father's at the Tulsa Junior College, from the eastern part of Ukraine where they speak both languages. He is tall and thin, with pale skin and smooth features. His nose is slightly crooked, which the girls find charming.

Everything about Sasha is charming to the girls. He has curly black hair and long eyelashes and scruffy black eyebrows. The girls like the way he laughs and the way he walks and the things he talks about. He teaches Zoe Ukrainian for half an hour and Amy Russian for an hour every Thursday from 3:30 to 4:00 and from 4:00 to 5:00 respectively.

Sasha is an energetic boy who always has something new to report to them about the outside world. Sasha stars in plays and plays in a band. To Amy and Zoe, Sasha might as well be Michael Jackson, or the President.

The girls compete for his attention, but there is no competition. Amy is almost thirteen years old now. She is almost all grown up. She can feel him watching her sometimes, and in these moments, she feels both thrill and panic, neither first, and she understands that she is in love.

Sasha's eyes are kind, and soft, and one time she gets lost in them and loses her train of thought and can't finish her sentence and turns bright red. The whole week between that class and the next class she spends blushing each time it comes back to her, which is all the time. She doesn't tell Zoe. This is the second secret that exists between them.

Amy spends hours studying Russian in their room with the door closed. Her favorite letter in the Cyrillic alphabet is ж, which looks like a butterfly and sounds like the s in treasure, zh. Amy copies out all the words from her pocket dictionary that start with ж.

Zoe is less diligent, preferring to play. Zoe rescues two baby squirrels from the street and names them Orange and Banana and dedicates her afternoons to feeding them and training them to become wild again when they are old enough.

Amy learns twenty new words per day and goes over all the old ones. She makes flash cards out of expired coupons and junk mail. Then in her spare time she plays Oregon Trail with Zoe, taking over whenever it is time to hunt the rabbits because the sound it makes when your shot is successful is the most satisfying sound in the world. Zoe claims it isn't fair for Amy to do all the shooting because in real life Amy stopped eating any meat at all, but Amy says that doesn't matter and leaves Zoe with no option but to relent.

Their mother tells Sasha that Zoe's memory got damaged in the surgery, but Amy knows the doctors said it didn't, and that it must just be the squirrels. She does not say so. She just gives Sasha a significant glance that she is sure he understands.

The girls get their periods within a day of each other

By now Zoe is ten and Amy is thirteen. Amy gets hers first, on a Sunday. She knows what it is and is proud of herself for knowing, but what she does not know is what to do about it, so she goes and finds their mom, who because it is Sunday is playing Dr. Mario on Zoe's Game Boy. Dr. Mario is like Tetris only with pills and viruses instead of blocks. Zoe doesn't play her Game Boy much because she's been so busy.

Amy clears her throat and whispers as loud as she can that she has her period and that she needs to know what to do. Their mom jumps up and leaves the Game Boy on top of the washing machine. This makes Amy feel important, and for an afternoon, Amy and her mom have something in common.

But then Zoe gets her period the next day while their mom's at work, and Amy has to show her about pads and split the stack their mom had given her and listen to her whine and cry about her stupid cramps. It is typical of Zoe to have to do things at the same time as Amy, in spite of their respective ages. Now she acts as though getting your period is worse than having your skull split open and your brain rearranged. Amy shudders to think what will be next.

In ancient Greece a clue *was just* a skein of yarn *until enough mythical figures unraveled their ways out of mazes.*

Amy sends secret messages to her sister that her sister can't read

She wants to make Zoe study more, but the plan backfires, and Zoe gets frustrated and threatens to give up.

Amy exchanges her first emails with Sasha. She pretends to have questions she doesn't really have. You have to be very careful typing emails because there isn't any way of going back to remove a wrong letter, you have to just start over if you mess up. It's a little bit like walking a tightrope over a gigantic canyon that will kill you if you fall. Amy tries to focus on the letters' bright green lines. She doesn't know how you send emails in Russian or if you can so she writes to him in English.

He always answers. This is the third secret that exists between Amy and Zoe, who thankfully is deemed a little young for emails still. Zoe loses interest anyway, after an initial outburst, and wanders off whenever Amy sits down at their mother's desk.

Sasha appears not to use capital letters, which lends his emails an air of the forbidden even though they are only explaining the difference between the accusative case and the genitive case for the hundred millionth time. Amy wishes she could write to Sasha about something else, but she can never come up with anything.

Winter comes early and cold. There is ice on the sidewalks, and the dog slips and falls every time they take it out. It looks funny with its stocky little legs that fly in all directions, but Amy tells Zoe not to laugh because it seems to her the dog can understand and feels embarrassed. Amy always ends up having to scoop it up in her arms and lug it home, even though it's dirty, although she doesn't really mind as much as she pretends to. It's nice to hold a living thing to you, especially a small thing like a baby or a dog.

Over the summer Amy perfects her knots

As it turns out she excels at canoes. She always lets Zoe go with her even though Zoe isn't very strong so Amy basically has to paddle by herself. Amy likes the way the water drops from the paddle onto her bare legs when she switches sides. It's lake water: dirty, cool.

At the end of each session there is a dance in front of the lodge or inside if it is raining. But it hardly ever rains at the end of a session. Amy wants to dance with the other campers. At first she tries, but she can't shake the feeling that everyone is watching her, and she can't. So Zoe doesn't dance either. She just sits beside Amy and taps her orange-and-black-striped tennis shoes against the hard bare dirt. Actually they're Amy's shoes, passed down, because the girls keep growing.

Their mother doesn't work there anymore, but she comes to pick them up and stays awhile talking to all the people she knows. One time on the way home she stops to save a couple of box turtles trying to cross the road. She puts them in a big tin bucket on the porch and gives them the scraps left over from lunch and dinner. But then the tortoises get maggots inside their shells from sitting in one place for too long, and they have to let them go.

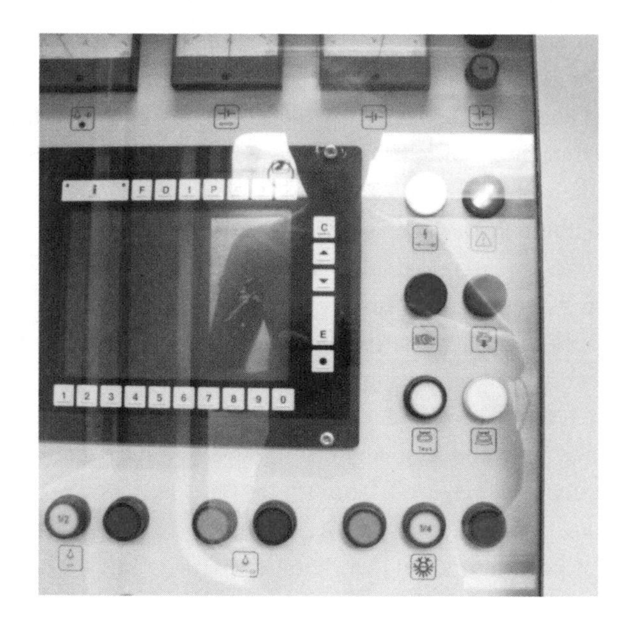

Words are worlds, with capacities enough for polar opposites, like left, *meaning* remaining *and* departed, *or* oversight, *both* supervision *and* failure to see.

There is an aisle at the MedEx that the girls never visit

One day it occurs to them that they could go by themselves while their parents are out. It is like when they learned how to read and worlds opened up before them: now they can't imagine why they never went before, although they can't remember what it was like before they went, either.

On this aisle they find pads for their periods and tampons, which is what they came to look at, but they also find things they'd never dreamed of, like intimate feminine wash, intimate waxing kits, and personal lubricant pumps. They widen their purview. They find condoms, pills for sexual fitness, pregnancy tests you pee on to see if you have a baby or not.

Speechlessly they agree to spend their savings on a box of tampons, a box of condoms, and a set of two pregnancy tests, one for each. Amy has more money because Zoe always spends hers, and anyway she gets three dollars less per month because she's younger, despite her protests.

Amy makes Zoe make the actual purchase, too embarrassed, standing by the door like their parents might walk in at any moment. Too excited to resent her sister, Zoe is effervescent on the short walk home, swinging the sack of contraband wantonly around. At home they rip apart the boxes and take turns examining the instruction sheets inside. They take turns peeing on the pregnancy tests. They discuss if they will ever really use the tampons. Ever since their mom explained what being raped was they have worried what will happen to them when they grow up. Their mom said if they ever did get raped they must remember the way her brother's girlfriend got freed without being murdered was to always look the rapist in the eye, which made him feel sorry for her, so even though he'd planned to shoot her, he did not. Their uncle's girlfriend said he said he planned to kill her, and he had a gun, which he raped her with, as well. Zoe asked how you can rape someone with a gun as though she understood all the other parts of the story. Their mom explained that the rapist inserted the gun into their uncle's girlfriend's vagina.

They peer into the diagrams on the instructions, how to insert it into your vagina. They don't know. It's more fun to pee on the pregnancy tests.

They empty out a doll case and stuff everything inside and put it all the way at the very back of their closet, behind their shoes. They cover the case in sweaters.

Their uncle broke up with his girlfriend because afterwards it was too hard. Their uncle died of alcoholism. Not suicide.

Of the apparently infinite quantity of delights offered to Amy by her recent forays into the garden of Russian grammar, the single most fascinating fact is that in the present tense, the verb to be literally goes without saying, so that in order to express, for instance, Amy is in love, you would only need Amy in love, or at most a dash: Amy—in love

Sasha is my teacher would just be Sasha—my teacher. Sasha is my friend would just be Sasha—my friend. Sasha is my boyfriend would just be Sasha—my boyfriend. I am Mrs. Sasha Doronyuk would just be I—Mrs. Sasha Doronyuk. And so on. In the past tense, on the other hand, and for the future, Russian offers no shortcuts.

The second most fascinating fact is that nouns in Russian get declined in the same way that verbs get conjugated—in the same way that I say but he says. These declensions are called cases. A noun's case depends on what its role is in any given sentence. This makes every sentence like a play. Sometimes the actor dog plays one character; sometimes it plays another. If I see the dog (собаку), it is declined in a different way than if I do something with the dog (собакою), talk about the dog (собаке), or if the dog does something on its own, like bark (собака). The result of this is that everyone's performance belongs so definitively to them and them alone that you no longer have to rely on any order in space or time to make a statement clear.

Amy memorizes the declensions with the same zeal she once applied and still occasionally applies to her Kumon. Amy loves clarity; Amy loves rules; Amy loves when things are perfect. Amy loves that in Russian there is a formal and informal way to address another person; Amy loves that she and Sasha use the informal way, even though technically he is still her teacher, and technically they do not know one another that well. Amy never realized how far removed she could feel from someone until she contemplated that formal form of address; now being close feels even closer. Amy loves that gender is always indicated; she gets excited when Sasha says an adjective that applies to her, in the feminine, as when he says an adjective that applies to him, in the masculine.

The laws of our world, like gravity, or time, do not apply in theirs.

During the Winter Olympics in Lillehammer the girls do nothing else

Riveted, they even manage to forget about Sasha for up to ten minutes at a time. Astonishingly, both girls win: Zoe, backing the Ukrainian Oksana Baiul, wins the gold in ladies' singles, while Amy, backing the Russians Yekaterina Gordeeva and Sergei Grinkov, wins the gold in pairs.

Uncharacteristically, Amy admits that her sister's skater did a pretty good job. She approves in particular of Baiul's performance to the Camille Saint-Saëns cello solo about the dying swan. Both girls find it so mesmerizing that they rewind the tape over and over and practice flapping slowly like Oksana, trying to see if they can get as graceful as her. They try and hold their legs up without using their arms. They try to do the splits.

Zoe's favorite part of skating is the jumping, and accordingly, she leaps around the house a lot. Amy's favorite part is spinning. In the swan performance Oksana Baiul starts spinning on one leg, bringing the other up from behind to meet her hands. Clasping her skate she forms a perfect backwards circle with her body and then leans in until the circle becomes parallel to the ice. She spins and spins. Amy closes her eyes and pretends that she is spinning, but you can't really spin on the carpet. Mostly she just stands like a flamingo, like she used to when she was a kid.

Nonetheless there is no one better than Yekaterina Gordeeva and Sergei Grinkov, who are perfect at skating and also in love and also the most beautiful people in the world besides Sasha. Amy wishes she could be just like

Katya and that Sasha could be just like Sergei even though Sasha is also already perfect. Yekaterina Gordeeva is the most beautiful woman in the world. She has a pure, simple face, with pretty blue eyes and smooth brown hair that is always pulled back. She is very petite. Amy would love to be that small. You could hide wherever you wanted and curl up much better.

The way they look at each other and how they manage to do everything at exactly the same time, even triples, and the way he raises her over his head, slowly, like he is relishing how much he loves her and like she weighs nothing, and the way she leans back like it has never occurred to her he could kill her if he dropped her on the ice on her head—everything about Yekaterina Gordeeva and Sergei Grinkov Amy loves.

Amy would like to become Russian. Russia is very far from Oklahoma, though, and Amy does not know how she would get there. She doesn't own a suitcase, and the allowance she receives from their parents is thirteen dollars per month. She knows her grandparents have a little bit more money, but she can't ask her grandparents, who don't approve of Russians.

Amy thinks and thinks without coming to any solution.

I guess I've thrown myself into my travels as though maneuvering through time as well as space, and flouting gravity.

Zoe still has seizures, but not as often as before, and when she does they aren't as bad

They're more like little twitches. Her eyes twitch to the right and her right thumb moves back and forth, and she moves her lips but can't talk. But then they're over, and she's okay, and they don't have to go to the hospital.

She still has to have her blood taken and has to get CAT scans, which now they call CT scans. The scans show the hole in Zoe's brain, which looks like a moonscape after an asteroid strike, as though the doctors used an ice-cream scoop to remove the tumor. Like when the Waluhili counselor got bitten by a black widow and kept space in her leg for secret messages.

Amy writes letters to all of Zoe's favorite celebrities and saves their responses for these moments, thinking if she can surprise her at exactly the right time, she won't notice the needles or the noises or anything else that scares her. She gets an autographed picture of Oksana Baiul. She makes their dad take her to the drugstore to buy a clear plastic frame for a dollar fifty so it doesn't get messed up. She thinks that this time it will work. But Zoe still gets scared and cries. Although then she spends a long time looking in silence at the picture.

Amy gets a typewritten letter from Viktor Petrenko and a handwritten note from Paul Simon. She tries writing to Dr. Seuss, but it turns out he has died already, the girls just didn't know about it yet.

The better Zoe does, the more their parents leave them at home alone and for longer and longer periods of time. The girls tape songs off the radio and choreograph dances. For a long time their favorite one is Salt-N-Pepa's Shoop. They puzzle over the words, trying to get to where they can lip-sync. Even when they can parse them out they don't always know what they mean. Zoe likes to say the line that goes, Lick him like a lollipop should be licked, but nearly four years before Monica Lewinsky, neither Amy nor Zoe could possibly fathom the actual thing that is being suggested. They just know it has something to do with sex, and this is enough to obsess them.

Zoe develops other problems, though, like allergies to all different things. One evening she becomes allergic to grape juice, and her mouth swells up. Their parents accuse Amy of hitting Zoe when they first come home. For a little while their mother stands up very straight and says that they can't leave Zoe alone with Amy anymore. Amy pictures stabbing their mother with the kitchen scissors, imagines the blood. She turns and goes to their bedroom and lies down. The dog goes with her and prowls around, sniffing at the squirrel cage.

Until today, I thought I would have given any-thing to change the way things went with Sasha.

Three things happen in 1995

Amy is thirteen and turns fourteen in September. Zoe has been ten since November.

The first thing that happens happens on the morning of April 19. The girls are setting up a house with their dad's old Lincoln Logs. The Lincoln Log is a kind of precursor to the Lego, just logs with a little groove at either end that lets them stay together. The set, which the girls discovered on a recent tornado warning in the hall closet at their grandparents', is in perfect condition, almost as though it has never been used. The only problem is that the dog keeps nosing around the base they've made, and Zoe doesn't want to put it outside.

Although not due home from work till lunchtime, their mother comes storming in at ten. Saying nothing, face flushed, she turns on the TV.

What remains of the Alfred P. Murrah Building looks like a body after a severed limb. Wires hang loose like snapped arteries in exposed organs, all the walls ripped off. Amy's hand hovers over the box she was reaching into for more materials when the image appeared. Their father comes in from his study. Their mother turns to him in a flurry of savage, desperate gesticulations. Her eyes are shining.

More than six years before September 11, the Oklahoma City bombing shocks the nation and utterly cripples the girls. Fourteen adults and six children are confirmed dead by afternoon. A photograph of a fireman carrying an infant with a blood-covered head is shown and reshown on every channel, printed and reprinted in every paper. The infant dies. Zoe won't stop crying. Amy's stomach churns. No one has even the slightest comprehension of what has happened. They spend the evening at their grandparents'. Someone is always on the phone with the cousins in Oklahoma City or the other ones in Texas and Missouri who also need to know. No one they know has been directly affected. But somehow that doesn't seem to matter: it might as well have happened in their backyard. For the first time ever, they all four spend the night at their grandparents' house.

The second thing that happens is the verdict in the O.J. Simpson trial. For this the nation is prepared. Domino's Pizza reports that in the hour before the verdict it receives the most orders ever in its whole history, but not a single pizza is ordered in the entire United States of America in the minutes between 12:00 and 12:05, central time.

Amy and Zoe watch the verdict at the Junior College, on a big TV screen in the middle of the Main Commons, where hundreds of students and some teachers have gathered and are sitting or standing or squatting waiting for the time. Amy and Zoe stand alone at a balcony on the second floor, outside the office where their dad is in a meeting, scanning the crowd in search of Sasha. A woman says we the jury in the above entitled action find the defendant Orenthal James Simpson not guilty of the crime of murder in violation of penal code section 187(a), a felony upon Nicole Brown Simpson, a human being, and the door behind Amy and Zoe opens up, and their dad comes out and sees he's missed it and says let's go, even though they haven't found Sasha yet, and they wanted to wave to him from the balcony, like in a fairy tale.

Between the Oklahoma City bombing and the verdict in the O.J. Simpson trial there is a summer of hummingbirds in the Roses of Sharon at their grandparents', of watermelons and watermelon fights into which Amy is dragged by Zoe against her better judgment, and of a perfect performance by Yekaterina Gordeeva and Sergei Grinkov set to Ella Fitzgerald singing a song called The Man I Love. This performance, and this song, will serve Amy for many years as the sole definition of love. The way she awaits him as he skates towards her, the way her face lights up when he gets close. Her immaculate plain beauty. How she can land smoothly on a single blade every time he tosses her into the air no matter how many times she spins around or how fast she is going.

How many times would they have fallen first to get everything so perfect? Or was it always perfect? They started skating together when he was fourteen and she ten. Did they always know they were in love?

Amy is certain that someday she and Sasha will be just like that. That if there is a period of initial falling, that that is the period that they are in now. But soon they'll get in sync together, and everything will be perfect.

But on November 20, 1995, the third thing happens. Amy finds out from their grandma, who finds out from the news and calls the house. It is so unthinkable that Amy cannot bear to think about it. To Zoe's absolute outrage, Amy throws away all the tapes they have of figure skating. She bans the topic from all conversation and will not tolerate even the slightest allusion to anything involving sports, ice, love, happiness, or beauty. Let alone direct invocations of Sergei Grinkov, who has died at the age of twenty-eight of a heart attack, leaving Yekaterina Gordeeva inexplicably alone.

Since Oklahoma City Zoe has clung on to Amy in her sleep. Her limbs grow heavier and heavier until by the end of the year Amy flings them off her in the middle of the night and threatens to make her sleep out in the hallway on a cot made of stuffed animals.

She turns away from her sister and holds her purple octopus in her arms. She remembers the boy at the hospital with leukemia who first accused Amy of cheating and who must be dead by now. She sleeps little. She hates nightmares, especially when they're true.

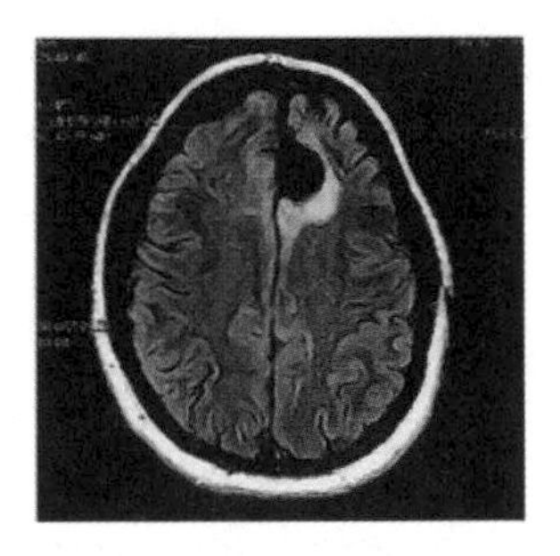

Sasha and Amy are reaching the end of their first-year textbook

The final chapter is titled What We Need for the Table. It teaches the dative singular and ordinal numerals. The dative plural and cardinal numerals they will get to when they get to the second-year textbook, though first they plan to spend some time on poetry.

The subchapters in the final chapter of the first-year textbook are Buying Groceries; Age; Expressing Fondness, Need, Uncertainty, and Desire; and Time by the Clock. Amy finds it impossible not to say something incriminating when she tries to use the dative singular in expressions of fondness, need, uncertainty, and desire, so in her homework, she focuses on food.

One day Sasha says he feels more at home at their house than he's ever felt anywhere in his life. He says it to their mother, but Amy knows it's really meant for her.

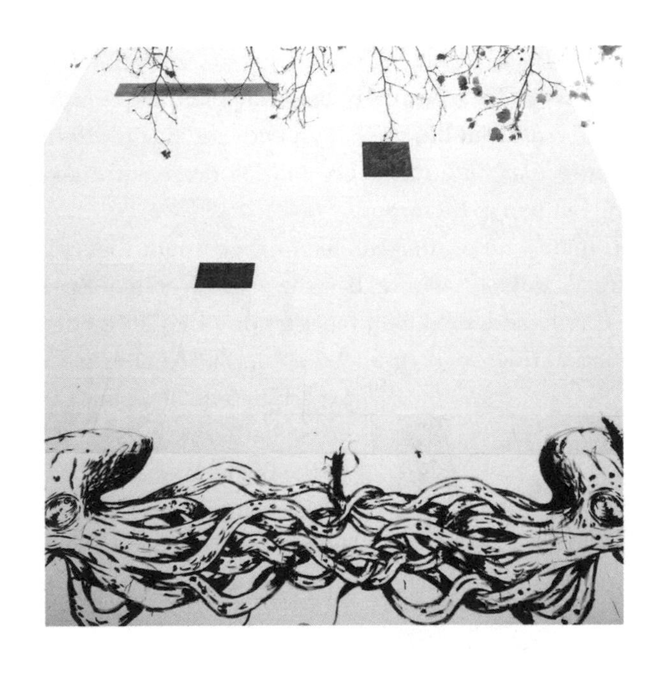

Do you remember when you used to always try
to hold my hand when we would go somewhere,
and I'd say no because even when we were little
I always thought we were too big?

Amy knows when Zoe lets the squirrels loose at last that her sister's secret hope is they will choose to return someday, but Amy also knows they won't

So she makes Zoe a peanut butter and potato chip sandwich, with the crusts cut off, and she spends the whole afternoon watching *Aladdin* and *Beauty and the Beast* with her and letting her win at Monopoly.

In the evening after dinner in their room they play a game called If Sasha Were. If Sasha were an animal Zoe says she's pretty sure he'd be a meerkat or a lightning bug or a Rhodesian ridgeback, or a swordfish. But Amy insists he'd be a bluebird. If Sasha were a constellation the girls agree he'd be the Big Dipper. If Sasha were an instrument Amy says he'd be the cello. Zoe says he'd be the drums. Amy says that's just because they know he plays the drums, which does not have any relation to what he'd be, but then as she watches the dog try to wriggle out of her sister's clutches, she remembers Zoe's just set Orange and Banana loose at Whiteside Park and will probably always be asking herself now if they're okay when it rains or gets cold or gets hot, a kind of concern that is new to them, so finally Amy says fine, he can be the drums, although inwardly she knows beyond a shadow of a doubt from the way he sits and how his face gets when he gets serious that if Sasha were an instrument, he would be the cello.

Amy wears perfume to Sasha's play

She retrieves a vial named Sunflowers from the shoebox in her fossil drawer and sprays it gingerly on her wrist, in the bathroom, with the door locked even though they're not allowed to lock the door in case what if they get electrocuted. She half expects everyone to make fun of her, but maybe she doesn't put enough on because nobody says anything on the car ride there.

Amy doesn't really watch the play. She waits for Sasha. When Sasha comes onstage the audience claps as though they've been waiting, too, and a bolt of jealousy shoots through Amy's core. It is fine for Sasha to have other friends, she thinks, but some of these people are girls. But now Sasha is talking, and his firm male voice, all-encompassing, eradicates everything else, even the words, which Amy's brain can't process. She simply listens to his voice, appreciating his thick eastern accent, but treating it all as music, not talk.

Amy watches Sasha's face. Sasha's face is taut, but open. Amy watches Sasha's hands. Sasha's hands are big, but delicate. She tries to think what their first kiss might be like. She would shut her eyes. Past this she can't imagine. She worries she will not be good at kissing. She watches closely when people kiss on TV, and she practices sometimes on her octopus in the bathroom with the door locked, but still.

Maybe Sasha can teach her the way he teaches her Russian. She hopes he will not make fun of her. Although maybe she won't be so bad. She hopes in fact that she will be a natural like she is at other things. That's what their grandmother says, anyway.

Despite the diagrams that came with the condoms they bought, Amy can't quite really believe that Sasha would have a penis. The idea of their whole bodies touching from head to toe appeals to her, but she can't even see herself naked when she attempts to envision it, let alone him. She likes to think that he will hug her when he graduates, to say a temporary goodbye, but then it won't be their whole bodies. It will probably only be between their shoulders and their chins, and then their hands will rest on each other's backs for an instant, though probably not more.

She feels guilty she has Sasha when she thinks of Yekaterina Gordeeva, who no longer has Sergei Grinkov. But she can't help it that she loves him, and she tells herself it's not her fault. She loves everything that Sasha's ever said and everything he ever will say, and everything he will ever do, and everything he's ever done.

After the play there is a party. Amy and Zoe stand in the corner shifting their weight from foot to foot. They are both wearing their church shoes. They don't speak. They just wait for Sasha to come out from backstage.

But then he does. He sees them first thing, and his face lights up. But Amy flinches: it feels too good to be true. She takes a tiny step so that she's shielding Zoe with her shoulder, but Zoe misinterprets it and thrusts her away, and Amy doesn't counter because she wouldn't know how to explain. And then he is there, holding Amy tight in his arms. She breaths in his cologne and the smell of his sweat and what smells like cigarettes although she knows he does not smoke, and other smells she can't decipher, and when she gives up she starts to pull away, but he still holds her, and she becomes aware of her chest pressed against him, and she pulls away, and ducks down a little, and he lets go.

Immediately she knows she's just gotten her period, and that there is blood running all down her legs. It is impossible to check and impossible to ask Zoe because they never successfully established any kind of useful code.

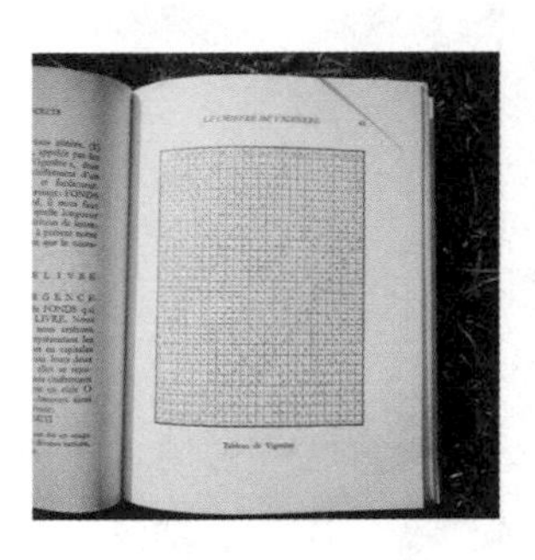

Amy sees their parents heading over and exhales. Sasha hugs Zoe, but it is not the same. Their mother wants to take a picture, but Amy excuses herself and goes to the bathroom.

There isn't any blood.

Afterwards as they cross the parking lot their mom says Sasha must have been drunk. Scandalized, the girls wait for their father to correct her, but he says nothing. Zoe reaches for Amy's hand, but Amy's fingers wriggle loose.

Except for Red Rover. Remember how we used to be the perfect team and nobody could ever even dream of tearing us apart? (This picture comes from near where we live now, in Argentina.)

Everyone in the family is aware that Sasha will be graduating soon

As the date approaches, they begin to consider what to do next.

Their dad has the idea of taking Amy to the community college, which offers Russian classes, too. But when they go to sign her up for one, the secretary says that first she has to take the SAT.

Their parents discuss. Even though the SAT costs twenty-three dollars, and their dad has lost his job again, they decide to let Amy take it. They sign her up for the next test date. She needs to score in the sixtieth percentile to be eligible to take her Russian class. Their dad says not to worry because the test is really for older kids, so if she doesn't score high enough, it doesn't matter.

But when her scores come back, they discover they are perfect. Amy is not in the sixtieth percentile, but rather in the ninety-ninth. This gives them a new idea.

Although few people do it, it is possible to go to college early, without even getting a GED

You have to have good grades and really good standardized test scores, and do well in your interview. Amy is a polite child whose taciturn manner—in fact a blend of shyness and mistrust—tends to be confused with maturity. She is admitted to the University of Tulsa and given a free ride, including room and board. She is what is known as a Presidential Scholar.

She is admitted to other schools, too, but nowhere else gives her a full scholarship. Besides, since she is only fifteen, their parents say she needs to stay close to home. And their parents like the University of Tulsa, the mascot of which is the Golden Hurricane, and now they always watch them playing basketball on TV.

Amy enrolls for classes.

She does not consider Zoe now, or the worry she might come to feel, her sister gone. She does not think of the fact that her own life is about to change forever and completely, or if she does, she thinks of that change only in terms of how it may affect her relationship with Sasha. Sasha will move away, but maybe he will visit someday, and by then she will be a college student, and she will know all the things you have to know in order to be a girlfriend. Then they may get married. Amy will wear high heels even though she will be taller than her husband.

She writes all this in unsendable letters to Sasha, which she keeps inside a shoebox, until one day she catches her sister poring over them when she thinks that Amy has gone to the living room to read. Without hesitation Amy rips the box away from Zoe with her left hand and punches her sister in the stomach with her right.

Zoe howls. Their parents come running. They find Zoe doubled over, crying, and Amy standing over her, fist still clenched. Amy braces herself. Yet she feels strangely indifferent, as though none of this concerns her any longer.

Then her sister surprises her by lying. She claims she just has cramps. That night Amy lies awake under their mother's mother's quilt, tugging the threads loose, watching the catfish suck at the small stones all along the bottom of the aquarium. Listening to her sister's steady, heavy breaths. She takes stock of the secrets between them: on her side, the secret stash of photographs that she still keeps; her secrets about Sasha, which now number in the dozens; her secret future; her secret grief.

Add the accidental secrets kept inside the labyrinths of signs and symbols Amy created to protect them from the world, all those notes Zoe refused to learn to read.

Subtract the secret rooms that Amy couldn't access at the hospital, where things were done to Zoe that Amy cannot ever know. Subtract the lies that Zoe might be telling Amy, too, in the same way that she lied to protect her earlier that night.

Did you know octopuses know how to communicate as well as camouflage by altering the colors and the textures on their surfaces, like magic?

The week of Sasha's graduation they have one last class

Zoe has been learning a Ukrainian folk song for the past month, practicing by singing it to the dog and her stuffed animals and whenever they're in the car and while she rides her bike. The song is about a girl who keeps promising to go on different dates with a boy but always stands him up. It starts on Monday when she says she'll pick periwinkles with him but doesn't end up coming. On Tuesday she's supposed to kiss him forty times but doesn't end up coming.

Ти казала в понеділок
Підем разом по барвінок
Я прийшов, тебе нема
Підманула, підвела.

Ти казала у вівторок
Поцілуєш разів сорок
Я прийшов, тебе нема,
Підманула, підвела.

The song goes all week, but Zoe can only remember those first two days and the chorus, which reiterates the extent to which the singer is tragically disappointed by his beloved's lack of interest.

Due to the fact that for them, all boys are Sasha, neither Amy nor Zoe is able to fathom how a girl could not want to go on a date with a boy. It may be because of this, thinks Amy, that her sister can't remember the rest of the song.

Meanwhile Amy has prepared a ten-page paper on her plans for the coming years. The assignment was actually to use the conditional to talk about what she would do if she won a million rubles, but Amy wants to show Sasha that she is not a child, and that instead of winning a million rubles she plans to earn some money and travel the world in the future tense, rather than the conditional mood. She has learned the names in Russian of nearly every country, along with the names of exotic fruits, animals that live in the jungle, and because she happens on a book about architecture at the library one day, she also includes in her essay some famous architects whose names she transliterates into Cyrillic whom she may commission to build her a house on one of the continents (whose names she also knows).

As always, she waits in the living room while Zoe has her lesson. While Zoe attempts to sing, Amy pretends to read. Then when it's her turn she presents him with her paper and looms over Zoe until Zoe finishes pretending to sort her papers and stands up. Then Amy gives her a look that makes her leave the room.

Sasha goes over Amy's paper as he always goes over Amy's papers, attentively, fondly, like a person playing a cello in the middle of a symphony. Amy can't always tell if he thinks she is impressive or if he thinks she is a freak. She is aware that she works harder for these Russian classes than what is expected. In her mind as he reads she traces his premature laugh lines, the circles under his eyes, thinks what it would be like to brush his face at the cheekbone with the backs of the lower thirds of the fingers of her right hand. She repeats the gesture over and over in her mind as he turns the page.

It is all going as it always goes, as she wants it to go, when all of a sudden an unthinkable occurs: Sasha starts crying.

He doesn't even cover his face. He just cries, heaving like water beginning to boil, tears splashing down all over her paper, diluting the ink, undoing letter by letter.

Amy thinks she may be having a heart attack. Her left arm goes numb. Her heart is racing. She will die on the thick brown carpet of the dining room before anyone even remotely thinks of calling an ambulance.

Then as though possessed by some unfamiliar spirit she rises and takes a single step towards him like she's gliding across a rink. She brushes the tip of her left middle finger against the back of his left hand. And in a flash he has seized her and is clutching her the same way the girls have clutched at their dolls and their octopi in their most harrowing moments of despair. Amy is on Sasha's lap, her left shoulder and her neck wet against his flooded face. He holds her so tightly she can't move, can barely even breathe, so she is spared the uncertainty of how to rub his back or pet him on the head. He sobs. Amy breathes him in, his briny musk, and what must be alcohol, and what must be cigarettes.

They hear the screen door get stretched back and then voices with the entrance of the key into the lock of the inside door. Sasha casts her off him and races through the kitchen to the bathroom. Amy hears the door lock. Their parents are in the middle of some conversation when they come in, don't notice Amy's wet shirt or face. Sasha reemerges a few minutes later seeming fine. But Amy doesn't really look at him. He leaves. She goes into the bathroom and takes the wet sea-green hand towel and brings it up to her face. She takes a deep breath.

Or that they have three hearts that pump blood made up of copper, rather than iron?

Amy does not mention to Zoe what has happened between Sasha and her

There are now too many secrets to keep track. This one she would like to tell her, to relieve herself of this burden, this complete incomprehension and this complicated fear, but something new has begun to be erected between them, something like a wall, and on Zoe's side it must stay safe, and on Amy's side it can't. Amy is responsible for repelling her sister as her sister tries to scale this wall. No matter how many boosts and footholds Zoe receives from their mother, who would rather there be more disasters.

Which is why when she lies to their parents about why she doesn't want to go to his commencement she lies to Zoe, too. She's almost even convinced herself she has a migraine. She spends hours in bed with the shutters drawn, lying on her stomach with the quilt kicked off, the octopus's eight arms draped around her shoulders. Striving for quiet.

It is their mom who breaks the news to them, one by one, Amy first

It is July 26, 1997. Their dad is in Minnesota filling in for a friend at the Summer School of the Rochester Community and Technical College. It is strange to think that their father has so many friends, none of whom they really know. Amy and Zoe have often wondered where they came from.

She tells her. Amy says oh the way she'd say it to someone she didn't know, like she means to say okay but forgot to finish.

Then their mother tries to give her a hug, but now Amy recoils, eyes bulging, blood cold. Their mother tries again. Amy pushes her away, hard as she can. Their mother staggers back, and for one split second, she doesn't seem to know what she should do. Amy stares and backs away.

At first, before she blames herself, she blames their mother. Then Zoe walks into the room, and Amy and their mother turn to her, and the three of them just stand there, in silence, and then Amy runs out.

Amy runs out the front door and down the steps of the porch. She runs down the sidewalk and then down the driveway. She gets to the street, and she keeps running. She runs and runs and runs all the way down New Haven until it ends. She is all out of breath now and has a stitch in her side, but she can't stop. She turns and does a dragging lope down a couple more blocks till she gets to Whiteside Park. She sits down in a swing.

She looks straight ahead of her and then slips out, sliding down onto the woodchips, with the swing sideways against the backs of her knees. She lets it go. She brings her knees to her chest.

Now it hits her, and she begins to apologize into the air, over and over: I'm so sorry, I'm so sorry, I'm so sorry. Because Amy is the one who did this. Amy is so lucky she brings others all the bad luck in the world. Amy has infected everything she's truly loved. Amy has poisoned them, and she should have known, and she should have done something. She should have done something. She should have done something.

How can it be too late?

As evening falls she tries to go home, but she has lost her sense of direction, and she drags herself down blocks that could be anywhere for what seems like it must be hours, until finally somehow she finds their long, squat house, the clumsy globs of gray between the rough red brick, and entering unnoticed she makes her way back to their bedroom and goes to sleep beneath their bed.

When we were kids I used to wish we could be octopuses, so we would not need words.

And we wouldn't ever even think about disasters, since we would just be textures, and copper, and water.

And light.

To get away from Zoe, Amy transfers all her operations to underneath the pear tree in between the front yard and the backyard

Amy still expects for Sasha to come back. Their mom is a liar who tries to hurt them on purpose. Amy does Russian homework all day long as though invoking him. The sun beats down and brings her freckles out, an endless succession of freckles, impossible to count. The wind picks up. Amy completes every remaining task in the second-year textbook and then starts over.

She sees Zoe at mealtimes but doesn't speak to her. She takes big bites of her food and then goes and spits it out into the toilet. She is on a hunger strike. She will not eat until Sasha comes back. At 3:28 on the following Thursday Sasha will knock on their door as though nothing has changed.

Amy and Zoe sleep stiffly, like strangers forced by some natural disaster to share a pallet. The catfish sucks at the small stones at the bottom of the tank while the little machine pumps oxygen into the water. The angelfish are too old now to lay eggs. They always ate them anyway.

Most of Amy's sleeping she does outside, under the tree, during the day. She dreams of Sasha. She dreams that he tosses her up into the air and catches her, and then they spin around and around and around and around, faster and faster and faster and faster, and then they hold hands, chests heaving, and skate back to the center of the rink to take their bow. Then she wakes up and screams inside and tries to fall back asleep.

Sometimes she claws at the concrete. Sometimes all her muscles tense up so tight she gets terrified because what if she can never move again. She listens to the cars go by and tests out her fingers and wraps her hand around her throat.

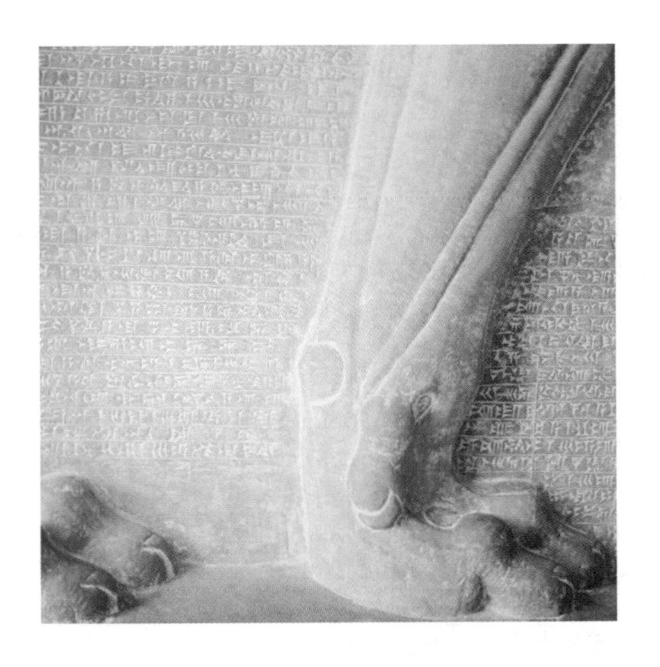

Remember how whenever we'd play Ring around the Rosie Mom would remind us that the lyrics were about the plague? But we pretended not to hear her because Ring around the Rosie was the best, and all you had to do was all fall down.

Because Sasha shot himself in the mouth rather than at the temple, they are able to do an open-casket funeral

Amy and Zoe scour their closet for something black to wear. They ask their dad to take them to the mall so many times he finally relents. Amy and Zoe scour the sale racks for something black to wear. They purchase dresses. Both of them are sure that Sasha will come back. That this event is an event he'll be attending, just like them. Thus they both want to look pretty.

People mill around on the sidewalk outside the parlor. Some of the college girls smoke cigarettes. Amy glances at Zoe, but Zoe keeps her eyes on the little bows at the toes of her shoes. Their mother walks ahead of them, puffed up, pushing through the crowd.

Inside some of the college girls are crying. Questions form in Amy's brain, horror and adrenaline surging through her body. Amy and Zoe know next to nothing about Sasha's life. Where is his family? Who are all these girls?

Then their mom works a space for them in the line to go up to the coffin. Amy goes first. She places a tidy pink envelope on his stomach just above his hands. Then she stands there and looks down at his face. His eyes are closed instead of sparkling. His hair is long, and she nearly reaches down to brush it off his forehead. Gripped by vertigo, she staggers back and hears, right before she faints, the sound of all things being torn in half, a resounding pulling apart that drowns out everything else.

Amy spends the next few days in bed as though she has a fever. Her sister ferries trays of food she doesn't touch back and forth between the kitchen and their room. She begins to lay down little notes beneath the juice glass. When Zoe isn't looking, Amy takes them and unfolds them. They are written in a shaky hand, using Russian Cyrillic or the symbols of the earlier alphabets that Amy invented. Zoe has recovered the marks without the meanings.

But even though the notes seem to say nothing, she begins to take sips of the juice, until finally one night in the middle of the night she gets up and rifles desperate through the fridge until she finds the big piece of leftover chocolate cake and eats it all standing up at the counter with a soup spoon. Then she feels sick, throws up and goes back to bed. Zoe is still sleeping.

On August 10, 1997, they move Amy into her dorm

The girls live on the second floor; the four of them trudge up the stairs carting boxes and garbage bags of things.

Zoe weeps. Zoe won't stop weeping. Amy would like to hug her, but she can't. She just stands there and waits for them to leave, and then when they do, she steps up to the window and watches them as they get smaller, trailing her fingers down the glass pane.

Remember how we'd all fall down and then do angels?

Amy lives in the Honors House, in the middle of fraternity row

The Honors House is a designated residence for participants in the Honors Program, otherwise known as nerds. But it used to be a fraternity house, too. It was converted in 1995 after one of the new recruits was accidentally killed during hazing.

There are not that many nerds at the University of Tulsa, so unlike in most of the campus residences, everyone has their own room. Amy has never had her own room before. She takes her few things out of their bags and boxes and lines them up on top of the extra bed. She is about to hide her valuables at the bottom of what is to become her sock drawer when she realizes: she doesn't have to anymore.

So she leaves her things lined up on the extra bed and makes her own bed and lies down. She does some snow angels, and then she lies still and thinks of Sasha in his coffin and begins to cry, silently, a skill she has perfected. She thinks of her sister's sadness, which redoubles her own. She cries until she falls asleep, wishing she had never wished for her own room.

The next day Amy meets people

Everyone is friendly, and no one seems so much older, and she doesn't tell them she's fifteen. But she doesn't tell them anything other than her name. When in the evening they all gather in the living room for their first official house meeting, Amy hangs back, standing in the doorway, watching them like you'd watch TV. They go around and introduce themselves officially and say their major; Amy's whole body is shaking by the time it gets to her. She almost whispers Amy, undeclared, and then it's even worse because she knows no one's heard her, and yet she also knows she has done the best she possibly can. She has the inexplicable sensation that trying again may kill her, although she couldn't say how. But just then the boy standing closest to her repeats her information on her behalf. She had not noticed him there, in the shadows. Now she looks at him with wet and thankful eyes. He goes on and says his name is Tommy and that he is doing a dual major in philosophy and German.

After the introductions, once everyone turns their attention to something else, Amy starts to take baby steps backwards until she reaches the base of the stairs. Quietly she creeps back up to her room holding tight on to the rail. Without Zoe Amy has no idea how she should be when she's with people, and no balance.

(This is a picture of several disasters: a ship-wreck at the bottom of what was once the Aral Sea, a harbinger of the emergency upon us.)

But the next day Amy becomes famous

She wakes up knowing she'll be in the paper. She showers quickly and gets dressed, heads fast across the campus towards the QuikTrip on 11th Street. It is early, and there is no one around. It is her favorite time of day.

Amy has never gone to a gas station alone before, and now as she glides along the asphalt of the parking lot and pushes in the glass door without slowing it occurs to her that now her life will be like this. That all she has to do is get the money and she can go wherever she wants. She approaches the counter where the Tulsa World is kept, and she pictures herself on Red Square. It is a Red Square with Saint Basil's Cathedral, the Eiffel Tower, a pair of tame rhinoceroses, and the Berlin Wall. She is standing very straight and looks the boy behind the counter directly in the eye.

Yet while Amy feels all-powerful at the thought of her name in the newspaper, when she glances down and sees her face taking up the whole top half of the front page, the power bursts, and she starts shaking, and she runs back to the bathroom, where she pees with her head in her hands.

In the front-page picture Amy's long blond hair rolls smooth as a single piece of silk over her shoulders

She wears an oversized coral-pink T-shirt she considers more dignified and a little amber pendant on a slender silver chain. Her eyes appear greenish gray, and she appears to be looking at the camera and looking away at the same time. She smiles without showing her teeth. Except for the slight sunburn on her cheeks and across her nose, she looks like a doll.

The headline of the article reads: Wonderkid Starts TU at 15. It starts by explaining that Amy is the youngest freshman in the history of the University of Tulsa. It goes on to include statistics from the U.S. Department of Education and interviews with the University of Tulsa's Dean of Admissions, Amy, and their mom. The Dean of Admissions is quoted in the second paragraph saying he would advise against anyone doing anything like this. The article's author explains that the issue is not so much whether Amy belongs in a college classroom as whether a fifteen-year-old belongs in a residence hall on TU's fraternity row. The Dean of Admissions again: We made sure she and her parents are aware of the maturity issues.

According to the U.S. Department of Education, says the journalist, the number of college students who are younger than seventeen has actually declined since 1970. The potential for that number to grow, however, is considerable. How many Amys are out there is anyone's guess.

Some people, Amy is quoted as saying next, underestimate their abilities.

A second, smaller picture on page A4, where the story is continued, shows Amy sitting cross-legged with all her books for the semester piled up on her lap: Antigone, Anna Karenina, Introduction to Marine Biology, and a bunch more whose titles are hidden by the ones on top. Her head is bowed as though she's reading.

Amy is described as reserved but articulate and not exactly shy. Physically, she could easily pass for seventeen.

When Amy reads this she wonders if it's true.

The article explains that Amy has been homeschooled for the past six years. Amy is quoted as saying, My sister had a brain tumor, and that made it difficult for her to go to school of any kind. I think my parents ultimately decided they might as well keep me at home, too.

Their mom is quoted as saying, We knew what we were doing was best for her. If anything this is the proof of that. We have raised Amy to be a strong and independent thinker, passionate about her interests, dedicated to achieving her future. At home she was able to focus in a way we knew she would never have been able to at school.

The article concludes with another quote from the Dean of Admissions: You just have to be very careful. If you go out trying to recruit younger kids, you can be doing a disservice to the students. It's got to be the right situation. We had a battery of campus personnel, ranging from admissions staff to faculty to housing staff, meeting with Amy and her parents. We'll see how things go. We certainly all wish her the best of luck.

If you stop and think of all the different things that could befall a living being—besides the modern shibboleths, besides more and more tornados, there are famines and tsunamis and shootings every day—you realize it's a miracle a single one of us lives for a single fraction of a second.

Zoe and their parents pick her up at six to celebrate

Amy skips out of the Honors House keeping her eyes on the car. When she opens the door and leans down to peer in at her sister, Zoe's strained face loosens, and then it opens up into a smile. Amy gets in.

Their grandparents always get everywhere early to be seated in the smoking section before their mom can say no. As they wind their way between tables Amy looks at boys and men. Their mom tries to speak Spanish with their guide; Amy and Zoe exchange a glance and roll their eyes as if on cue. But their mother sees, and blushes, and sinks down into her seat defeated, looking off into the distance at what must be nothing.

Their grandma, on the other hand, is ecstatic, halfway through a margarita, and she takes Amy's face in her hands and gives her a quick wet kiss on the lips. She keeps repeating the word Wonderkid even after they've placed their order. She starts to tell stories the girls have never heard, about when they were too little to remember and Amy was always figuring things out on her own. Their grandma's cigarette floats above a basket of tortilla chips, perfectly parallel to the table, half ash, and Amy can't not watch it, waiting for it to snap in half and spoil the chips, knowing just what their mom will do when that happens. But it doesn't snap, it lingers, as if by magic, and then as she starts a new story their grandma takes it down and taps at the ashtray, and Amy breathes out. There was the time the crazy neighbor climbed the tree in the backyard, says their grandma, and Zoe and their mom were watching the TV. And Amy had been instructed, she was not to move, and yet regardless, just when everything seemed over, and out the window the ambulance drove off, slow, and then the fire truck, just then: bam!

Their grandma claps her wrinkled hands together; Amy jumps. Their dad is smiling like he wants to laugh; their mom is still looking off into the distance like she's not listening. Zoe looks at Amy. Amy looks back at their grandma, who beams. Amy'd slid right out from underneath that bed and crept around the side of it and grabbed that gun. Their mom always claimed it was an accident, but they had always known different, because it could hardly have been accidental, because Amy was just that kind of kid.

And Amy is left to wonder what kind of kid she'd been, and whether or not she is the same kind now. Their grandma stabs out her cigarette and says, Shot clean through the window! And she turns to look Amy square in the face, looking like she might cry from happiness, clasping Amy's hand and holding it high above the guacamole.

Amy tries one last time to catch her mother's eye. Their mother, who is the one they've heard this story from so many times, is the only one who has the power to make this total overhaul make sense. Amy with a gun? Amy shooting out a window? What if she had shot her sister? What if she'd killed Zoe? How could she have known what she was doing when she was only four years old, when even now, at the age of fifteen, she has no clue?

But their mother suddenly recoils. That man over there is looking at your legs, she says, looking off still but jerking her head in Amy's direction. Amy sees that her face has turned bright red. I'm going to go over there, she says, and her voice is thick. You're fifteen years old. That's called statutory rape.

Their mother is rising from her chair. The girls glance together, stricken. Their dad reaches out and says, Leslie, but she shakes off his hand and has launched. There is a little pause like everyone's lurched forward. Oh forget it, says their grandma then. Let's order more margaritas.

The girls gaze down at the remnants of tortilla chips in tiny triangles that slip into the scratches in the thick, glistening wood. They try to keep from hearing their mother's voice across the room.

Oh Zoe. Remember the copper roofs in Copenhagen that Dad had in his atlas, that pretty green they turn?

Back in her room Amy peers out the window listening to the music that resounds from downstairs

It is the moments between day and night, when things are pink.

Because their grandma insisted, Amy has had a little bit of alcohol—her first. There is a slight warmth to her now, as though time were a ball to be kicked around.

And then she is going to the party, hand in hand with the girl from across the hall, who seems to know how everything works. Amy is wearing her own jeans but a tank top that belongs to her new friend, satin spaghetti straps like a bra's and lace along the top, trying not to look down to make sure her breasts don't show because she'll get dizzy if she does.

When they walk into the Lambda Chi house they are greeted by the boys like old friends and presented with red plastic cups that foam over in their hands. Amy looks at Katie and takes a sip. Inside the Lambda Chi house the music is so loud you can feel it in your feet. Amy's heart adjusts to it, beats in time. The smoke obscures the slow shapes she can make out in the low light, but Katie seems to see better, and Amy lets her lead her into the middle of the room.

The music is the music Amy's always listened to, with Zoe, and now she notices in a rush of pride and pleasure that she feels just like she feels at home, and Amy and Katie dance, drinking foam from their red cups, and when their cups get empty, as if by magic, they get refilled. Never before today has Amy been the beneficiary of so much kindness, and she stumbles over thank yous now, unable to convey her appreciation. But the boys don't mind. The boys just smile. Amy rocks her hips and sips at the beer and thinks it's like she's been whisked off by a tornado and set down in Oz: the rules are different, or there are no rules. She smiles and turns to Zoe about to say so, knowing Zoe will nod a bunch of times like whenever she gets excited, an enthusiasm that reveals even the silver fillings in her back bottom teeth, but then she sees that it is Katie, not Zoe, and she takes another drink.

Boys come, one for each, and Amy feels swallowed up, vanished, safe. Although she must have been held as a baby by someone, she has no recollection of it, no conscious knowledge of what it feels like to be inside of an embrace. Except for Sasha, heaving, crying, and she finishes her drink. The boy she is dancing with takes her by the hand to go and get another. She drinks another, dances, drinks. Why did Sasha take her that time on his lap, and why did he hug her, and why and how had she not seen? Amy drinks. Amy drinks and drinks and dissolves and is happy, being held.

Katie comes and takes her hand and guides her down some stairs. In the basement are more people, other music, bottles instead of cups. Amy is given a bottle and says thank you with tears in her eyes. Oz is amazing; ever since she grew up she has been happy, Amy thinks. Next she will be a woman who lives in Europe, with Zoe, and they will buy a boat and visit all the islands. Katie is talking to someone now, and Amy can't hear, so she looks around. There is a semicircle of girls with bottles on the other side of the room, and Amy looks at each of them, having never been a part of a crowd like this before. She knows she must be imagining it, but she thinks they are looking at her, too. A jolt and her eyes dart down to Katie's tank top, strap to strap, but it's fine, that isn't it, and she looks up again, relieved. But now it's spread. Now there are girls and boys just watching her, talking to each other leaning in like telling secrets and glancing at Amy in the pauses.

Amy wants to run away but can't without Katie: she isn't sure she can find the front door from here, and she also isn't sure she isn't too drunk to go anywhere because suddenly her legs can barely hold her, and in terror she drinks more. She reaches out and taps at Katie's shoulder, a light, polite tap, and then when Katie doesn't answer she yanks her to her by the wrist. Katie tells her it's just the paper thing and that they'll get over it, and then she twists her arm away and returns to her conversation.

Everyone understands everything except for her. Amy strains to decipher Katie's words. The paper thing? Amy thinks of their grandma's story. How could she have known what she was doing when she was only four years old? She doesn't even know now. Now she doesn't even know what is happening right in front of her face. How can it be too late? thinks Amy, but then the same boy who spoke for her at the Honors House meeting comes up out of nowhere and says, Hey, you're famous.

She blinks at him and then remembers. People are worried the cops are going to come, says the boy, and she thinks his name is Tommy. Tommy leans in very close to her face. Now some other boys come slowly towards them, smiling, asking all kinds of questions like how does it feel to be a genius and will she help them with their homework and won't her parents get upset with her for hanging out at parties.

Amy answers what she can: her parents won't care.

The boys ask if Amy has a boyfriend. After she says no Amy wishes she'd said yes. Then some girls come up and say shoo, and the boys dart off in all directions like flicked flies, looking back over their shoulders now and then. The girls ask if she's okay or if she wants to go home. Amy thinks. She says she's fine, but then she thinks because she does want to go home, but then she also wants to dance again with a boy and get held. But then she thinks that maybe now she's famous she'll be too watched to dance, and she'll feel like a fish in an empty aquarium. Plus now, if they know who she is, she can't pretend she isn't who she is, and who she is is a person who shoots out windows and brings everyone bad luck. Who she is is a person whose sister gets sick, whose heroine's perfectly healthy husband has a heart attack at the age of twenty-eight, and whose—but who was Sasha? What was Sasha to her?

How can it be too late?

So she says goodnight to Katie and lets the girls take her back up the stairs. Tommy comes up again—out of nowhere, again—and announces he can take her from there because he lives in the Honors House, and he knows which room is Amy's. The girls look at each other, but now Amy needs to throw up, and she starts out the door without waiting.

Once in a while there is a word with no translation.

Amy doesn't know exactly how to be in class

Her memories of before her sister got sick, when they still went to school, are unreachable, tiny dots on the horizon of her mind. She is not exactly daunted; she has reason to believe she will be good at these things. All she has to do is sit like the other kids sit and always scribble in her notebook so no one calls on her. It's just it is the opposite of teaching Zoe all those years.

Some of the other kids sit up straight and smile when smiled at, while others slump back in their seats and look serious or neglected or sleepy, or something—Amy's not sure what. Amy cycles through the different postures, trying them on. She is so unused to being exposed to people's eyes around the table that there's no way she can listen to her teachers. It takes up all her energy just to sit.

Russian, which was the reason Amy came here in the first place, now sounds like screaming into a hole gaping into the ground.

People go in packs to the cafeteria, where you can pick

whatever you want to eat and eat as much as you want. All of this is included in Amy's scholarship. For a while she eats only desserts and drinks only fruit punch mixed with Mountain Dew, but then Katie says she needs to eat something resembling real food or she'll give herself diabetes.

There are five of them from the Honors House who do everything together: Amy, Katie, Tommy, Vijay, and Hoffman, which is a last name, but for some reason everybody uses it instead, like they do sometimes on TV. Vijay is majoring in pre-med, and Hoffman in petroleum engineering. Like Amy, Katie is undeclared.

The boys call Amy Wonderkid, and it is the first time she has ever had a nickname. Having a nickname makes her feel like she is part of something too big for her to be able to see, and the resulting sense of smallness reassures her. And besides, the way they say Wonderkid makes it sound like they are proud of her, like she's their little sister. It's fun to be a little sister because you don't even have to make decisions, you just get taken wherever everybody else is going or watch whatever everyone else is watching. They get to watch TV until as late as they want. Amy watches them watch TV, and when it's something scary, Tommy covers her eyes at the worst parts, or Vijay does, if he's sitting closer.

She talks to Zoe on the phone every day before they go to dinner and tells her what her homework is for tomorrow and if she saw anything funny and age-appropriate for Zoe on TV the night before. Zoe tells Amy about the stupid stuff their parents say and says she wants to go to college, too. She keeps on saying she might be coming down with something because her body hurts like when you're getting the flu, but then she never actually does get sick, so Amy doesn't know. She's worried their parents can't know how to care for her, and she wishes Zoe could just come and live on campus, too, although she knows she is too young. And she does have faith in Zoe's doctors, who have encountered nothing new in any of her test results.

The pack goes to parties whenever there are parties, which is Thursday and Friday and Saturday for sure and sometimes other days. Protected by the pack, Amy is immune to her fame, and the initial flood of questions about the article in the Tulsa World dwindles down to a trickle, then dries up. They dance and talk and mostly drink till late. If the next day is a weekday Amy likes to look around the classroom and see who all she saw the night before, and when she sees someone she tries to exchange a glance with them like they are in a fellowship of red plastic cups, and it pleases Amy, too, that now the tables have turned, and it's the adults who aren't in on it: for all their teachers know they stay in studying, when in fact they are all only pretending because actually everyone is hungover, secretly miserable, just like her.

Such untranslatables may be my favorites—although, at the same time, with their bridges always drawn, they also make me feel (to use a word you used to use) forlorn.

One of Amy's classes is Photography I

It has been a long time since she last took a picture. Now she rediscovers the world.

She takes walks and takes pictures. The University of Tulsa campus is mostly sandstone with a little limestone and slate. Amy photographs it at night, using walls and benches as tripods. During the day she goes up 11th Street and photographs the gas station and the Taco Bell and the Taco Bueno, the pizza places, the Coney I-Lander—her grandpa's favorite hot dog place—and the Arby's, with its gigantic cowboy hat sign that says Arby's ROAST BEEF Sandwich IS DELICIOUS. She does the Metro Diner, which is so easy to photograph Amy later almost wishes she hadn't: the neon sign that says ELVIS EΛTS HERE, the turquoise padding on the booths, the cherry-red vinyl on the chairs at the tables. The checker-print wallpaper, the jukebox, the silver Art Deco M on the door. When she shows these in class she knows it seems like she is making some kind of statement, something in between attack and affection, and she feels uncomfortable.

She keeps going down 11th Street. She photographs the dumpsters in between the drive-thrus and the restaurants' wood fences, the American flags in all the parking lots, and the cars, and the semis. She tries to catch the contrails of the planes that pass overhead, but often they elude her. She wonders what it might be like to take pictures in a place like Moscow, or Paris. She can't imagine it, though, and she keeps going, down the cracked streets, Florence Place,

Florence Avenue, photographing the compact one-story houses, many white or robin's-egg blue, with lengthy driveways and ample, screened-in porches, the maple trees and the dogwoods and the Roses of Sharon, but since it's already getting to be winter, there isn't anything in bloom.

Right around campus there isn't a whole lot more than this, so she gets Tommy to drive her around to other neighborhoods. They drive down Cherry Street and visit Swan Lake, Philbrook, even Gilcrease. They go downtown; they go to Weber's Root Beer Stand; he buys her a root beer float. Amy feels uncomfortable, because she doesn't have enough money to buy him anything later on. Instead she helps him with his German vocab every time he has a test. Then again this doesn't really count because Amy enjoys learning new words in any language, and she sometimes does the same for Katie, before her Spanish tests.

Tommy is clumsy, and sometimes when they walk he hits her hand with his hand. Sometimes he stares at her, but she doesn't say anything because she wouldn't know what to say, and anyway, she needs him now.

Forlorn—*the word you'd cry into the door of our bedroom when I would shut it in your face (although now I wonder where you got it from)—is the past participle of a verb extinct for centuries that used to mean* to part with *or* be parted from, *a close relation of the German word* verloren, *meaning* alone *and* lost *and (sometimes)* doomed.

The day of the Lambda Chi luau
Amy takes a picture of the pack

On the outside are Hoffman and Vijay, Hoffman with his furry arms and puffy hands protruding from his high-contrast Hawaiian shirt, Vijay with his hair slicked back and his sepia-toned jacket sleek and all the way zipped up. In the middle, Tommy and Katie, Tommy wearing what he always wears, an old gray T-shirt riddled with holes, his belly hanging down an inch or two beneath the bottom. His beard is sparse and scruffy; his mustache is just a few sprouts across his upper lip. Here he has a pea-sized pimple on the right side of his mushroom-shaped nose. Katie is skin and bones, her dyed-black hair straight down in the back, her face blank, her arms hanging along her sides, her palms to the camera. Her shoulders are slightly shrugged. Her lips are slightly ajar. It's an action shot, Amy tells her, when she complains.

One Wednesday in mid-November Amy comes home from class and finds Zoe making a fort out of the desk in her dorm room

When Zoe sees her sister she stops what she is doing and just stands there staring for a second, and then she bursts into tears.

Amy looks around. Both beds have been stripped to provide for the fort. On the inside Amy swells. She sets her backpack down on the cheap gray carpet, gets down on her knees and enters the fort. Zoe follows.

Ever since Zoe ran away from home their dad comes to visit at the Honors House, trying to broker an agreement between Zoe and their mom

Amy supervises these meetings, experimenting with her face and carriage as she attempts to convey the maximum amount of disdain.

There are just a few problems with Zoe living with Amy now. The first problem is that Amy does not want Zoe to see her drunk because Zoe's only twelve, although her birthday's soon. But after just a few days Amy misses the parties like she's lost whatever all she gained by growing up, and she debates what to do with Katie, who is the only one who knows about Zoe. Some of the other girls have seen Zoe, like when she has to go to the bathroom, but she has been instructed to say she is just visiting. Katie knows the truth and helps Amy smuggle food out from the cafeteria, which is another problem, because it's hard to feed a kid on dinner rolls and sugar cookies and impossible to transport vegetables in one's pockets.

The other thing is Zoe keeps on being in pain like she'll get the flu but keeps not getting it, and she is running out of the Tylenol she brought in her bag she packed to run away from home. And they don't tell their dad, but she is having seizures, too—worse and worse ones, more and more often. They don't tell their dad that Zoe's heart keeps racing, either, sometimes even waking her up during the night.

The other thing is Zoe misses the dog, which makes her get tempted sometimes to hear their father's nonsense, even though it is clear he is on their mother's side.

The good thing is that Amy reads her textbooks now, to Zoe in the evenings, to keep her entertained. There are so many things they can't talk about, like Sasha, that all of Amy's undone homework turns out to be a blessing. The best is the Introduction to Marine Biology, which they are doing chapter by chapter, in order. But just when they're about to get to the part about octopi, which they have both been looking forward to, Zoe has a seizure she can't come out of, and although every muscle in her body strains against it, there is something else in Amy's brain that makes her call their parents. And just like that they drive right up to campus and carry Zoe off in their car.

They say the Portuguese saudade *is a springy double helix of bereavement and relief over a missing person, place or thing (although they also say they can't really explain it using words besides* saudade*).*

On Thanksgiving at their grandparents' they have turkey and stuffing, rehydrated potato flakes, and cranberry sauce slid straight out of the can, with the grooves still in it, jiggling

They have sweet potatoes with marshmallows, which Zoe can't eat because sweet potatoes look like orange homemade Play-Doh, which made her sick once when she ate too much of it when she was little. Zoe does eat, on the other hand, the entire bottle of aerosol whipped cream, spraying it directly into her mouth. The crime is not discovered until it is time to eat the pumpkin pie, and by then the stores are closed. Zoe does not get in trouble now, but no one is particularly happy.

The girls watch old Cary Grant movies, each curled up with their heads at opposite ends of the couch, their feet almost but not touching, and it's all right, but Zoe laughs and cries too much. Amy says she has homework to do, and Zoe says so does she. Amy rolls her eyes. Zoe bursts into tears.

On the day after Thanksgiving their dad says he has an announcement to make. They are back at their grandparents' eating leftovers. They put their forks down and look at each other and then at him. Although it's been a hard decision, says their dad, and Amy's sure he's going to say that he and their mom are getting a divorce, but looking at her mom it doesn't look like that, so then she wonders, and their dad clears his throat and says, I have decided to accept a job in Minnesota, at the Rochester Community and Technical College. It's too good of an offer to pass up, he says, and the best part of it is it has full medical for all of us, and the hospital in Rochester is one of the top ten hospitals in the whole world.

In the hush that follows, all the things on the earth come unstuck and fly off into space very fast. Amy sees Zoe off in the distance against a deep dark sky, smaller and smaller and smaller.

They put the house up for sale

The girls learn the square footage and that the name of its style is ranch-style, like the beans their dad heats up to serve with grilled cheese sandwiches, which is the only thing he knows how to make.

Strangers come and wander up and down the hallways. Amy looks up from studying for finals and looks at Zoe, but Zoe is always too busy watching the strangers to look back.

Amy spends more time with her family, always returning to the dorm in the evenings, for parties or TV. Since Amy's had her license for a couple of months now their dad lets her borrow his car. Once backing out down their long driveway she crashed into their mom's car because she was listening to the radio loud and didn't hear their mom when she pulled in and started honking. Their grandparents found it funny and said it just goes to show what they mean when they say that most accidents happen close to home and that most murders are committed by friends and family. Their mom did not find it funny and said she shouldn't get to drive anymore if she was going to drive like such a lunatic, but then with all the stuff about the move, she seemed to just forget.

Whenever they go anywhere now they notice their house when they come back, low to the ground, brick, with all its greenery and sidewalks. The cool cement of the porch hidden from the street by the bushes with the tiny, waxy leaves.

The people they sell to make only one demand, which is that they cut down the big tree in the backyard, since inspection has shown it to be what they refer to as a structural threat. In spite of the girls' protests, their parents assent. So one day as Amy is about to leave some men come and climb the tree and start hacking off its limbs, limb by limb, bolts of thunder when they hit the ground.

And there is no single word in any other language that means the same thing as the Welsh hiraeth*, which I'm told is a refusal to surrender what has already been lost (akin, but not identical, to* homesickness*).*

A lot of their stuff they're getting rid of, whatever they no longer need

Most of their old toys and clothes they take in their dad's car to the Salvation Army. Their My Little Ponies, most of their stuffed animals, the little red suitcase, the dingy fake metal frame with the picture from The Wizard of Oz. All but a few smaller fossils Amy returns to the ground. The arrowheads she keeps.

They excavate from beneath the pile of abandoned sweaters the doll case that contains the condoms they bought some three years before. Zoe starts to open it. But to Amy, the spirit of the contraband has been transformed. Once fascinating, funny and disgusting, now the contents of the case are like a distant horizon abruptly thrust forward, like something irrelevant that suddenly makes claims.

As they evacuate the home that carried them through childhood, lead lines on the walls like little cracks made by how tall they were on every birthday, Amy becomes aware for the first time of having had a family.

She thinks of their mother's story about the girlfriend who got raped by a rifle. She thinks of Sasha in his glossy coffin, his ghost-white face made up by the morticians, no longer his, already rotting.

She snatches the box away from Zoe.

Zoe whines. Zoe won't stop whining.

In comes their mother. And Zoe stops. She looks from face to face like she doesn't know who to be more scared of.

In the spring semester, Amy takes Russian Conversation, Russian Poetry, English Literature Prior to 1800, The French Revolution, and Photography II, which is her favorite

Even though Russian Poetry is taught by a famous poet named Yevgeny Yevtushenko, Photography II is her favorite. Poetry makes Amy think of Sasha.

Amy likes taking pictures. But what she really loves is the lab. She goes at night when no one's there. You have to arrange it all before you start, anticipate all the steps, because then it's dark, and you can't turn the lights back on. Amy is good at anticipating the steps. You have to lay out the film canister, a bottle opener, scissors, the reel, and the developing tank, in that order. You have to space them evenly so you don't accidentally knock anything over and lose it on the ground somewhere. Then you turn all the lights off and use the bottle opener to pop the bottom off the canister, and then, carefully, you pull out the film.

You pour water in for one minute (Amy counts to sixty), and then you drain it and pour in the developer all at once. If the developer is too hot or too cold, it will mess up everything. Knowing this exhilarates her, makes her heart race. Once you have poured the developer in, you shake the tank gently for thirty seconds and then for five seconds every thirty seconds until it's done. Then you drain the tank and rinse four times with stop bath. Then you put the fixer in, and then the hypo-clearing agent.

Then the film is negatives, and delicately then you hang them up to dry.

The next day you make the prints, and the best part of everything is when you slide the white paper into the tray and gently make the waves of solution wash over it, back, forth, back, forth, and slowly, slowly, the image unfolds

You do have to be careful because photographic paper is expensive, and you can't waste it.

Being in the lab reminds Amy of being in the cave at the Tulsa Zoo with her sister. The cave was fake but still a little slimy, and they would chase each other through it, squealing at the slime and the bats and snakes they pretended they could sense, lurking in the clammy dark. Which was almost as fun as the earthquake machine, which was as fun as the rides at the State Fair. When there wasn't anyone waiting they would ride it over and over again, one hand on the padded railing, Amy's other hand over Zoe, just in case.

Then you have to cut the mats to the right size and frame the pictures. Amy gets frustrated cutting the mats. She sits on the floor of her dorm room trying to get everything perfect. One night her hand slips, and the box knife slices into the base of her other hand, eliciting a steady stream of blood. Amy looks at her hand, motionless. As she watches the mat turn red, her disgust blooms into something else.

This gives her a new idea.

Not people die but worlds die in them

Amy reads the poetry of Professor Yevtushenko. Her favorite starts by saying there is no such thing as boring people, that in fact every single person in every single place is so fascinating as to be unfathomable, and when they die, all of what's unfathomable dies with them: not people die but worlds die in them. She sounds the words out to herself in her dorm room, quiet as she can, tracing the rise and fall of the letters with the tip of her right middle finger.

Людей неинтересных в мире нет.
Их судьбы—как истории планет.
У каждой все особое, свое,
и нет планет, похожих на нее.

А если кто-то незаметно жил
и с этой незаметностью дружил,
он интересен был среди людей
самой неинтересностью своей.

У каждого—свой тайный личный мир.
Есть в мире этом самый лучший миг.
Есть в мире этом самый страшный час,
но это все неведомо для нас.

И если умирает человек,
с ним умирает первый его снег,
и первый поцелуй, и первый бой . . .
Все это забирает он с собой.

Да, остаются книги и мосты,
машины и художников холсты,
да, многому остаться суждено,
но что-то ведь уходит все равно!

Таков закон безжалостной игры.
Не люди умирают, а миры.
Людей мы помним, грешных и земных.
А что мы знали, в сущности, о них?

Что знаем мы про братьев, про друзей,
что знаем о единственной своей?
И про отца родного своего
мы, зная все, не знаем ничего.

Уходят люди . . . Их не возвратить.
Их тайные миры не возродить.
И каждый раз мне хочется опять
от этой невозвратности кричать.

At the end of the poem the poet rages against the irreversibility of death, the impossibility of restoring the people that we lose. One day in class Amy looks up from her book at him as he paces before the board: a rare moment of abandon, arisen from her nighttime readings. Professor Yevtushenko catches her eye. Amy feels the blood flash across her cheekbones. Professor Yevtushenko stops talking mid-sentence. The world turns black around the edges, and in her terror all she sees is him. You will be very beautiful, he says. But you must wear lipstick. Amy laughs, and her vision slowly relaxes and expands. Professor Yevtushenko is sixty-five years old, but his face is young except for the depth of his laugh lines. His eyes are bright and full of play. Red, he says, gaze sparkling. Red lipstick.

And he returns to his unfinished discourse on Russian railways.

When you consider the plenitude of any word's experience you might think all words are untranslatable.

Amy agrees to go to a youth group meeting with Katie without knowing what exactly youth group meeting means

They drive and drive, over the Arkansas River, out of Tulsa, southwest. They enter and then pass through Sapulpa. Katie talks the whole time, slapping the steering wheel, jostling the clump of keys lolling out of the ignition, turning up and down the radio, swerving. Katie is a terrible driver, but Amy doesn't care: she has a friend.

At around ten they arrive at a big powdery gravel parking lot overflowing with SUVs and red and blue Chevy pickup trucks. They squeeze into the only spot there is, and since there is no space on her side, Amy scooches over and gets out on her friend's. Once they're out they hear bellowing. Amy looks in the direction of the vehement voice and sees a thousand people packed into a square off in the distance. She glances at Katie thinking maybe Katie will want to just go home, but Katie is already heading towards the people.

Amy follows, and when they get there, Katie says something to one of the security guards, who lifts a rope up to let them inside the square. Amy follows Katie deeper and deeper into the people. She holds her breath. The minister is saying spitfire, unconnected things: Laziness is the difference between the five foolish virgins and the five good ones; The fire is being turned up and that is exactly the way it is supposed to be as we head toward the return of Christ; Blessed are they that do His commandments, that they may have right to the tree of life, and may enter in through the gates into the city. For without are dogs, and sorcerers, and whoremongers, and murderers, and idolaters, and whosoever loveth and maketh a lie; our position of zero tolerance for homosexuality, same-sex marriage, abortion or murder, fornication, graven images or idols, women or Jezebel preachers.

There is a split second of silence. Then he reads: And the Lord said unto Satan, Hast thou considered my servant Job, that there is none like him in the earth, a perfect and an upright man, one that feareth God, and escheweth evil? and still he holdeth fast his integrity, although thou movedst me against him, to destroy him without cause. And Satan answered the Lord, But put forth thine hand now, and touch his bone and flesh, and he will curse thee to thy face. And the Lord said unto Satan, Behold, he is in thine hand; but save his life.

The crowd erupts in cries and hollers, people raising their right hands and dancing around as though there's music. Amy is frightened and glances at Katie, but Katie has fallen down on the ground. Amy reaches down to help her, but Katie pushes her away. She talks, but Amy can't understand her. It's like when her sister had her first seizures, and Amy can't know what to do. Sweat floods her armpits and her thighs. She starts to take her coat off but can't maneuver with all the people around. She bends down again to try and hear what Katie is saying, but the language they once shared has turned to quicksand. The boy beside her grapples for her fingers. Amy rips her hand away and takes a step back trying to keep herself from sinking, jamming her heels into someone else's toes. She whirls around to say she's sorry and hits the boy beside her in the side with her arm. He takes her by the shoulders, shakes her, explains: Katie has received the Holy Spirit holy spirit of the Lord, and that's why she is speaking this way, in tongues. It is a blessing.

Amy, dizzy, knows that she will faint. She frees herself from the boy's grasp and takes one last look at Katie and begins to force her way back out through the crowd. The closer she gets to the edge of the square of people, the more air she is able to take in. But the security guards come together and won't let her leave. They say she has to wait until it's over. Amy looks at them, from face to face, and then she gives up. She passes out. When she wakes up she is lying in the bed of a truck with a stranger holding her hand. She has to pee. She is overwhelmed by the desire to urinate, infused with a sudden strength; she hops out of the back of the truck and runs across the parking lot and pulls down her jeans and pees leaning back against a dirty old silver Cadillac. Her coat conceals her, mostly. She sinks down lower and lower to the ground, repeating after the minister, quietly, then almost silently, like an echo, Behold, he is in thine hand; but save his life, and then it's over, and she pulls her jeans back up and fastens them. She finds Katie's little Honda Civic by the bumper stickers and slumps down against the left front tire and waits, teeth chattering, although she isn't really cold.

Zoe has been diagnosed with systemic lupus erythematosus, which explains the pain, and hemochromatosis, which is a genetic mutation that prevents her body from processing the iron it takes in, and they also think her brain tumor might have started growing back

For the lupus they prescribe steroids, an antimalarial, and codeine for use as needed.

Amy hangs up the phone and sits cross-legged on the cheap gray carpet. She cracks her hand down on the floor.

Amy prays without believing, bartering with the void. She will give anything. She will give everything. I'm so sorry, she chants into her hands, please save Zoe please save Zoe please save Zoe, she whispers into the hard cheap carpet, please save please save please

I wouldn't know how to translate homesick, *either, without sacrificing something, like the clash of its component parts.*

Amy has never liked to shower at the Honors House, but now it hurts

She hates it because you have next to no privacy, just a flimsy curtain anyone could pull open by mistake. She hates it because the suds from your shampoo collect at the drain and slime up everything. She always tries to be quick. But now she has to be careful. The hot water makes the cuts on her wrist sting from where she has been practicing. She tries to find a way to wash her hair without getting her wrists in it but can't.

One night Tommy hears her crying and comes into her room to ask if she's okay. He offers to drive her anywhere, and she thinks and pulls herself together and says, Let's go to the liquor store, because tomorrow is Sunday, and they will all be closed. Tommy has a fake ID. They buy three bottles of vodka. He buys them. He says she can pay him back later. She knows she will probably never pay him back, but she doesn't care: she needs the vodka.

According to their mother, suicide is the most selfish thing you can do

Amy weighs this against the certainty that Sasha was perfect and that everything he ever did was perfect. At the funeral, Amy overheard one of the college girls saying that Sasha had spread a tarp out over his bed so that he wouldn't get any bloodstains on the sheet. He had done it in the middle of the night but held a pillow over his face thinking that way the gunshot wouldn't wake his roommates, although it had, although it hadn't mattered, because he was already dead.

One thing Amy gets tripped up on is how come Sasha didn't leave a note. In Amy's understanding, suicides left notes to say goodbye and to explain why they were leaving. Without this explanation, no one will ever know what made him go, and that question will scrape up their insides like a swallowed fish hook, forever.

Amy cannot bear to think about Zoe, or how she feels.

For the millionth or trillionth time, Amy asks herself why Sasha started crying that day after their last class, and why he killed himself. For the millionth or trillionth time, she runs through all the scenarios she can possibly think of. None satisfies.

For a while she cries in bed, but then she starts to suffocate. She gets up and quiets down. She can't think of anything to do besides shots. She starts on the peppermint vodka she hasn't tried yet. Then she goes outside and sits on the front step and smokes a cigarette someone gave her at a party that she didn't use because she never really smokes. It gives her a headache.

She walks in circles around the House. The grass is wet.

She watches MTV all night after everyone else has gone to bed. She falls asleep around dawn and misses all her classes. It doesn't matter.

She thinks of Sasha: how they never heard him play the drums. Amy thinks he would have been good at dancing. She wishes she had seen him dance.

When we were kids I was so focused on making up our secret languages I never even wondered what I'd tell you if it worked—let alone what you had to tell me.

One night, in the middle of the night, Amy sneaks downstairs to the living room in the Honors House to take the rest of the cough syrup samples

She finds some samples of some migraine medication, as well. She takes everything, stuffing it into her backpack and then dumping it back out on the floor of her closet.

Katie's door is cracked open when she walks by. She doubles back and peeks inside. Katie and another girl are sitting on a bed with a mirror covered in white powder balanced between their laps. Amy looks at the other girl trying to figure out who she might be, and Katie looks up and leaps up and almost knocks the mirror over, but the other girl grabs it in time, spilling little.

Katie grabs Amy by the arm and pulls her into the room and slams the door shut. Her friend shushes her and eyes Amy and then looks back down. Katie pulls Amy towards her and asks, in a whisper, if Amy sees the insects. Amy pulls back and looks at her friend, brow furrowed, and now she sees that her friend is scratching at her arms and her neck, and that there are bloodied welts all over everywhere where her skin is bare. Amy looks into her face, which is scratched up and drawn. Amy does not understand, and Amy does not know what to do, or say. For a moment she just stands there, and then Katie lets her go, and she goes back over to the bed and sits down with the other girl. Amy looks at them, and then she goes back to her bedroom.

The next day, when Amy gets back from her classes, there are people coming out of Katie's room when she walks by, holding boxes. She doesn't see Katie again.

All evening Amy thinks of things she has to talk over with Katie. Outside the lag between these thoughts and the remembrance that her friend is gone now she's not capable of any kind of motion. She drinks and grips the box knife in her fist.

That night for the third night in a row she does not call Zoe. Amy knows she is responsible for other people's pains and disappearances. Like the time she tried playing with the children at the hospital, who all lost at Chutes and Ladders because she won.

It will be worse for Zoe if Amy sticks around. She hurts people, and doesn't help them, and she can't help it.

Amy knows that to save Zoe she must sacrifice herself.

What I never saw before was all the secret languages we always had already, the made-up names of things, and the real names of the features of our lives I see from here were specific to a time and place shared only really by the two of us: the highways we drove on and the meals we ate and the stories we were read;

Amy knows it is time for her to go back upstairs to her room now, but she is afraid

She has so many nightmares now that she wants to stop sleeping, forever. Sometimes at night she goes and sits in the closet thinking sleeping sitting up with the door shut might help, but it doesn't. She has tried sleeping everywhere: on the spare bed, under her own bed, on the floor in the corner, under the desk, on top of the desk curled up into a little ball. It doesn't help.

Being awake is even worse. Amy thinks of all the times she sat alone with Sasha in the dining room talking about pets and hobbies and furniture and food. All those times she could have told him not to do it. Maybe all he needed was someone to hold his hand and to tell him not to do it. But she did not do that. She just sat there, an idiot, a miserable, disgusting, worthless, useless idiot. And now he is dead.

So she keeps on drinking in Tommy's room, taking shots with him at first and then continuing alone out of a big plastic cup, slumped against his Nine Inch Nails poster. The short coarse carpet chafes against her legs through her pajama pants. She repositions herself. He is playing computer games. The door is open. Someone stops by. She doesn't say anything for fear of slurring her speech. When they leave, Tommy shuts the door.

Amy simultaneously wishes that Zoe were there and rejoices that Zoe is not there. She wants to set a good example for Zoe. This is not a good example, she knows. She knows she should go back up to her room now and try to go to sleep. But she is afraid, and when Tommy offers to let her have his lower bunk, she says yes.

Tommy is supposed to take the upper bunk. But at some point, after she has been asleep for a while, he sits down on the edge of the mattress where she lies curled up around his pillow. He cradles the nape of her neck in his right hand. She wakes up, sort of.

It has been a long time since Amy gave any thought to losing her virginity, or to her first kiss

She is startled by her own body once it is bared. She looks down and sees that she is very pale and so slight she is barely there, like a ghost, and it gives her vertigo.

Now she can't quite keep track of what is happening. When he takes her hand and puts it around his penis, she thinks it undulates, slithers, like a snake. Amy stiffens, and then she detaches from her body, watching the rest from overhead.

Afterwards she passes out again. She dreams of Sasha.

At dawn the next day Amy calls her grandparents, who are annoyed to be awakened but who come to pick her up and take her home with them

She goes upstairs when they get there and lies in bed all day listening to the sirens of the ambulances heading up to the hospital and the birds in the backyard. She thinks of when she and Zoe played rock-paper-scissors and how Zoe used to try to cheat, how mad she used to get at her. She follows the cracks in the ceiling with her eyes. Water over eons wears through rock; every summer the girls would look for proof, stones without centers like negatives of islands, like the one their mother had, but of course they never found a single one.

When they turn the news on downstairs, Amy rolls over and covers her head with a pillow, but she can still hear it. She thinks about the fairy tales their grandma used to read them, how scared they'd get. How frustrating it was that Hansel's path back home didn't lead anywhere. She scoots out from underneath the pillow and turns over again. She watches the ceiling until it begins to get dark.

Suddenly seized by something, she picks up a pillow, wrings its middle, and hurls it against the wall. She thinks how Anna Karenina lay down in front of a train. How Vronsky tried to shoot himself in the heart.

and the way we'd loop back to one another in every story that we told—the answers to each other's questions (even unasked—even unimaginable)—like the intertwining spirals of our common DNA.

In the middle of the night, Amy sneaks downstairs and takes her grandpa's car keys from the big ceramic bowl in the hallway and drives east

In the headlights the tar marks on the roads look like the splatters after animals. But Amy only thinks about where she is going because she doesn't want to get lost. She keeps the map of everything illuminated in her mind. She reaches the cemetery after about half an hour, and she drives straight to his grave. She turns the car off and slides down onto the ground. She shuts the door on her arm, forty or fifty or sixty times, trying to work up a bruise. She lies down on the ground, and then she gets up and gets back into the car. The windows in it are automatic, and she thinks how if they drove off a bridge in a car with automatic windows she might not be able to get them down in time to get out and save Zoe.

When she gets home she sneaks into the downstairs bathroom and carefully pops open the bottle of painkillers her sister left at Christmas. With the pills in her fist she tiptoes back up the stairs. When she turns the corner for a second she thinks she sees Zoe. But then her eyes adjust, and it's just a pillow lying crooked in the bed.

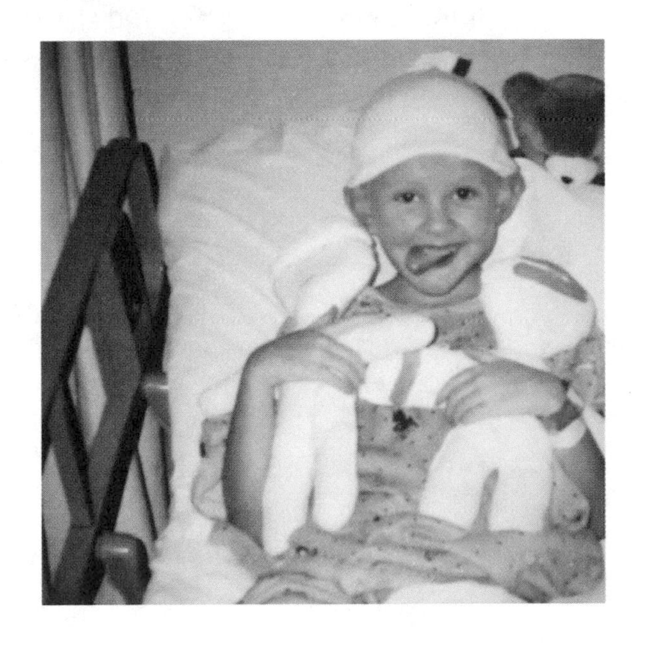

Every word is untranslatable if what translation is is making something new that stays the same.

On Monday, Amy can't speak Russian anymore

Her brain has changed. In class the letters wriggle out of her grasp and swim away. Amy realizes the world has ended for her now, and she can't keep going to her classes. She considers going to the cafeteria for a piece of chocolate cake, but she discovers she's too tired, and she has a big task ahead of her.

She tries to write a letter to her sister

As she struggles to summon any words in any language, she drinks all the little bottles of cough syrup, hoping they will help her know what she should say. But they don't help her.

She starts to write about nothing—about the weather, about how dumb their parents are, about how much stupid homework they have—but she crosses it all out and wads up the paper and tosses it in the basket by the door. When she is done with the cough syrup, she starts in on the rest of the vodka. When the vodka is gone, she takes the pills.

She is wearing jeans and her best long-sleeved shirt, which is red and has a pocket on the left side and three buttons down the front at the top made of abalone shells.

For the first time since she moved into the Honors House, Amy takes her shoebox out and opens it. She looks at the pictures of Zoe, from before her surgery, at her raucous eyes and her flaxen hair all specked with leaves and grass. She wishes she had taken a picture of Sasha—even one. She wishes she had let their mother take a picture of the three of them after Sasha's play.

There is the yellow string he brought and played with during an early class, and then forgot about and left behind. Amy never knew what it was or why he'd had it. But she kept it in her shoebox, and now she rolls it back and forth between her fingers. Then she takes a small scrap of paper with Sasha's handwriting on it and folds it up and clutches it in her right hand. Then she takes the box knife and begins to work at her left wrist.

It isn't easy, even though she has been practicing. The vodka helps, and the cough syrup, and the pills, but it still hurts, and her skin wants to resist. Amy begins to feel very tired. But she keeps on trying.

But that's not what translation is.

Amy wakes up in a white room with a minister who is holding her hand

Her eyes fight to stay open.

Cradled in her other arm, filthy now, its tentacles worn down to hard nubs of fabric, is Amy's octopus. She knows she tried not to get any blood on it. But she also held it to her and buried her face in it and stayed that way as they carried her down the stairs of the Honors House and out the door, and she can see she ended up getting blood on it anyway.

Amy tries to get out of bed but finds she is tethered to machines

She tries to count to ten in Russian, and then to twenty. The nurses have left a curtain half drawn, and she can see a clock that says eleven. It doesn't say if it is day or night.

Amy doesn't know what to think about except for time and numbers. She can barely even keep the numbers in her head.

She tries to imagine her sister sitting somewhere just outside her section of the hospital, like Amy used to do when it was Zoe inside, a coloring book black and white in her lap.

A sudden burning exhaustion knocks her back onto her pillow. She counts: раз, два, три.

She wakes up and sees her mom standing over her and flinches, and then her mom starts yelling

Amy wishes she was dead.

A nurse wheels her down to the thirteenth floor

They come to two sets of locked doors. The nurse presses the red button on the intercom, and together they wait. After a while something buzzes, and then the doors give, and then the first nurse hands Amy over to a second nurse and walks away.

Amy has been transferred from Pediatric Intensive Care to Adult Psychiatric, where minors are still allowed to come. Now Amy expects to see Zoe at visiting hours; this is how she makes it through the long first day. But when she returns to her room after art therapy, she finds, instead of her family, just a sea-green plastic basket on her bed, with a note in their mother's labored script.

The basket reminds her of the wild strawberries their father would take them to gather for their mother every May Day, but this memory disperses quickly, and Amy picks up the note.

We tried to bring your Sunflowers perfume, she reads, but they say you can't have glass. Here's your homework. We're driving back to Rochester today.

Back, Amy repeats after her mother, mouthing the word without pronouncing it. But that means Zoe doesn't want to visit.

For a second she is dizzy. She focuses and makes the room return. Underneath the basket are some papers, and inside there is a bottle of shampoo they must have taken from her dorm room, a new tube of lip balm, a washcloth with their grandfather's initials and a cracked off-white sliver of soap. Amy shuts herself inside the bathroom. There is no lock, so she piles her drawstring pants and tunic up at the base of the door.

Naked, spindly as a spider, shivering, she catches a glimpse of her grimy body marred by cuts, bruises, and the residue from bandages and patches as she tiptoes sideways past the mirror. On her tiptoes she steps onto the tiles in the shower box. She throws up as soon as she starts the water, from the heat. But she is determined to be clean. With the toast she ate for breakfast a scummy halo at her feet she scratches at the circles of paste on her chest and the marks on her arms and digs shampoo tracks in her hair. She scrubs. Her wrists don't hurt. Now she turns around and shuts her eyes, lets her heels come down, and the water washes over her neck and her shoulders, and she just breathes. She's not weak anymore, and after lunch they take away her wheelchair.

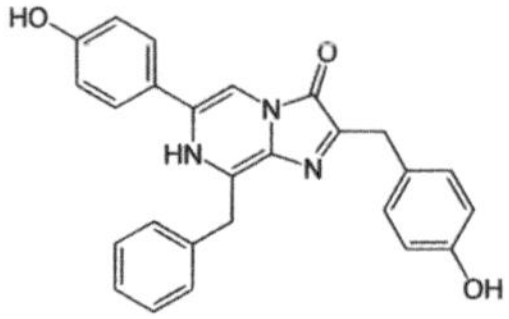

Remember when we used to swing dance to that song from the Olympics? Remember our routine? You used to back away a little and crouch down, and then you'd leap into my arms, at the very very end. If you tried to leap into my arms now you would probably kill us both, which means we really are too big.

She starts with her Russian homework, which is just her favorite poem by Yevgeny Yevtushenko, the briefest of instructions clipped to the top: Translate into English

Her eyes get wide, and she releases her shoulders. She clears her throat.

But only for the old things.

There are no boring people in this world

Each fate is like the history of a planet.
And no two planets are alike at all.
Each is distinct—you simply can't compare it.

If someone lived without attracting notice
and made a friend of their obscurity—
then their uniqueness was precisely this.
Their very plainness made them interesting.

Each person has a world that's all their own.
Each of those worlds must have its finest moment
and each must have its hour of bitter torment—
and yet, to us, both hours remain unknown.

When people die, they do not die alone.
They die along with their first kiss, first combat.
They take away their first day in the snow . . .
All gone, all gone—there's just no way to stop it.

There may be much that's fated to remain,
but something—something leaves us all the same.
The rules are cruel, the game nightmarish—
it isn't people but whole worlds that perish.

Each time a Russian word meets an English word it generates a spark. And translation offers Amy a new kind of math, an alternative to the math of sacrifice that has ruled her life on her own until today. She can't cancel out another person's suffering or death with hers. What she can do is connect.

It will take Amy many years to truly learn this. But this poem does provide a start. Amy has a hazy vision of herself as phoenix, rising in an unknown land (in truth she pictures a flamingo, fledgling, slightly stooping as it scrabbles), and she knows she has finally found some solution, and she sobs freely, with relief.

The thing is there are new things, bigger things, more miracles—worlds. Did you know that eighty-five percent of plant life lives in the ocean? I bet even combined we haven't seen half a percent of what can live on land.

PART TWO: HOME

People say the world will end when midnight strikes December 31 of 1999, but Amy has come to hope it won't, and then it doesn't, and then she graduates from the University of Tulsa and she flies to Berlin

She is eighteen, it is June 1, 2000, and the world's unfolding and in bloom, and it belongs, in its entirety, to her.

When she alights at Tempelhof she shakes her wrists loose as she hurries out into the airport as though she knows where she is going—and in a way, she does: tomorrow she will take the train to Moscow, and in Moscow she'll become a whole new person—luminous, herself.

She finds the baggage claim and claims her luggage—an old off-white suitcase of her grandma's, from before suitcases had wheels—and navigates the throng of those awaiting the arrivals of their relatives and friends. Her terror she will hear her name's in vain: in leaving Oklahoma, Amy has freed herself of nearly everything and everyone she's ever known.

Soon the room gets lighter, and she begins to hear the street. From inside the inside pocket of her jacket she extracts the grayscale map she printed in her grandpa's den. She holds it high, up to the light from outside like it's amber—and sure enough, the city glows, most around the page's perforated edges, the current limits of her expertise.

Yet just beyond her grasp, she sees trees quivering in gleaming sheets of glass, and closer, as she lets the map drop, people flicker past, their certain steps seeming to keep the flecked and polished floor in place; these gliding silhouettes all intermingle like the languages she hasn't learned or hasn't learned completely yet, which rise and fall in flurries.

In all of this activity, in all this mystery, in all these intersections, Amy can sense the nearness of the world's quickening pulse, and she can feel her own rising to meet it.

An hour from now she'll struggle with her grandma's suitcase until finally the clasp gives and slices right into her knee. At the abrupt unplanned eruption of her blood, Amy will faint, and when she comes to, she will find that the shards from her one picture frame have pierced all her packets of cheese and peanut butter crackers, and that all her cans of Dr Pepper have exploded in the air, staining her clothing—though she won't mind, starting from scratch, with just another little scar.

Tomorrow, without the right visa, she'll get kicked off her train to Moscow in the middle of the night in Minsk, and in Warsaw, have her head shaved by mistake—though she won't mind: she's always wondered what it would be like, or what it was like for her sister.

Between now and when she starts to write the letter to her sister, Amy will turn disasters into pictures, taking portrait after portrait of all the times she winds up lost and finds out something new about the world. In country after country she will calculate exchange rates and learn words, lie when she's missing the words for the truth and be lighter in translation because all words without memories are beautiful and hollow like the eggs Amy and Zoe used to dye each Easter that Zoe always tried so hard to keep from breaking.

Amy won't get homesick. She'll buy hats and a backpack and think about her sister as her hair grows back. At the grocery store in Warsaw, as she checks out, she will get yelled at for putting her fruit and yogurt in a plastic bag. In advance of the impending cold, she'll try to buy new clothes but get shooed out of the changing room for reasons she can't understand.

She'll study Polish. She'll get a Polish cell phone. Her Polish cell phone will get stolen one afternoon from the table where she's sitting having fuchsia soup. She'll get another Polish cell phone.

The brown-black walls of her apartment will seem to hold the cold, and the quiet will be so intense sometimes she won't know how to think when she wakes up. One day she won't remember the Polish symbols for men and women and will accidentally see a man standing over a urinal with his penis in his hand. One day she'll forget to pick up a basket when she walks into the grocery store, although all she will have wanted was some gum.

One April day it will get so slippery along the sidewalks that Amy will stop to break her walk up. She'll duck inside a coffee shop, where she will see a sunflower head the size of a wall clock flat atop a table by a window. A girl will hover over it, effaced by a burst of curls. As Amy stands dripping in the doorway, the girl will snatch seed after seed out, devouring them one by one.

Amy will travel to Wrocław and Dresden and Prague. She'll sit at stations for hours on end on purpose, never uttering a word. Enchanted by the whoosh and bustle all around, electrified by all the destinations that come up on the boards beneath the big clocks all the stations seem to have. In motion, time will defer to space; it will be the only time when everything is out of Amy's hands. There will be nothing that she has to do and nothing that she even can. It will be a carelessness that isn't careless, merely the absence of concerns. And for more than a decade, it will be the only way for Amy to be perfectly at peace.

Come summer she'll get thrown off her bus to the Baltic for not having a ticket for her backpack, propped up in the seat next to hers like a person. She'll pay her first real bribe.

The bus will still drive off without her. And as it drifts off the horizon, Amy will close her eyes and wish that she could have her sister back, nearby, but when she opens up her eyes again, Zoe won't be anywhere in sight.

So she'll take a picture of the serpentine slope of an overpass that won't capture the sounds of the cicadas or the bitter fragrance of the rapeseed fields, or the eddies of dust at her ankles or the sun that looses rivulets of sweat that pool around her throat.

Until Amy finally writes to Zoe, she'll tuck the old manila envelope that holds their shared history under her pillow every night. Pictures of a snail's shell; a felled spruce; a spiral staircase; padlocks on the Pont des Arts.

Speckled with Dr Pepper and peanut butter grease, punctured here and there by broken glass, Amy and Zoe at the playground, Zoe on her shoulders, her smile more like a scowl.

In the back of the ambulance, the whites of Zoe's empty eyes.

The envelope will bulge, and crumble at the corners, but Amy won't stop adding images to her collection as she moves from Poland to France to Germany to Argentina and falls in love again and wants to tell her sister but doesn't know how and travels and makes her way home again to the home she has made with her boyfriend in Buenos Aires—until one day, on a translation residency just outside of Kraków, she realizes she now has everything she ever wanted, and that it's not enough.

So she'll go back. Not to what could never be her home again, in Oklahoma, but rather to the runways where her world began.

Amy will imagine all the photographs there are and all the photographs there aren't of Tempelhof, no longer an airport now—some from before it was a refugee camp, before it was a park, before it had a concentration camp, before it ever even saw an airplane, when it held Prussian parades and, earlier, Knights Templar, when it must have been replete with bison, spruce bark beetles, hedgehogs, storks. Storms that split the sky with light and tiny yellow flowers that popped up from softened soil.

But right now, on June 1, 2000, she just folds her map up, tucks it back inside her pocket. She glances down at her grandmother's suitcase, glimpses a trickle of dark liquid emerging from its closest corner; hastily, carefully, she lifts it, then sets off.

Remember when you said that Sasha'd be a swordfish or a meerkat or a lightning bug or a dog, and I said he'd be a bluebird?

You were right, of course.

The thing is we were both right.

One day Amy wakes up wanting

It is June 1, 2018. She has just won the world's largest translation prize in London. The good thing is her dad is still around to be proud of her, although he's had leukemia for twenty years; with her mother and her sister she is barely in touch. Following the ceremony, Javi went to Paris, to teach a few classes, and Amy came here, near Kraków, to translate something new.

Outside the sun is shining; the snails are slinking down the sidewalks in their mobile homes. For the first time Amy comprehends the pleasure of pure want—what Zoe must have felt as she made lists for Santa—and she showers quickly and is dressed.

Many of the snails get crushed along the sidewalks; as she walks a little stooped from the weight of her backpack she bends down further to inspect their shells. Often they're in shards or finely ground now, the animals inside them just some sludge the shade of leaves left over from last fall. Amy shuttles the intact ones over to the other side, placing them in tiny clearings.

On the train hushed seas of green flash by with bales of hay like buoys, blanched cropped wheat.

All of us are anything, everything, brimming with secrets.

The breeze at Tempelhof is gentle

Now the runways have been overtaken by bicycles with brimming baskets, the asphalt itself burst through by stalks and blossoms, the once-white lines that guided planes now green, glittering when struck by sunshine.

Amy settles in a patch of cut grass, extracts the envelope. Slowly she unspools the red thread of its clasp.

A little yellow butterfly flits overhead.

From above, what the pictures most resemble is their mother's mother's quilt, made half of scraps and half of Amy's grandfather's blue uniform, ragged in the middle of one square from the night that he got shot and killed. Amy wonders how to tell this story to her boyfriend, how to explain that it's that very gash that makes it sacred, but then she wonders if they even have such things as quilts in Argentina—or if they have them here in Berlin.

Although it's easier to tell the stories of her childhood in any other language, Amy does encounter frequent obstacles like these.

As she searches her vocabulary, Amy's eyes move back and forth across the images, verifying their positions. It occurs to her that laid out step by step like this, more or less in order, the pictures also form a kind of path. This path strikes her as urgent, as though it's made of bread crumbs and can only be traveled down right now.

The breeze picks up. Quickly Amy gathers up her pictures, making a stack, more or less in order. Then she flips the first one over and embarks upon her letter. Pen trembling at first.

Above all we are the shelter we seek out in others and the safe havens we become for those we choose to love.

There is a picture of an insect in the yellow fronds at the center of a big white flower; in the background a dozen giant wet green leaves, flat and sometimes ragged at the edges

There is a picture of a single white azalea, half in shadow; in the background the red splotches of some other plant. There are pictures of pansies, and goldenrods, and Queen Anne's lace. Of hyacinths Amy can smell when she sees again, Indian paintbrush, and violets, and irises, and yarrow, tiger lilies and lilacs and phlox. A spikelet of wheat inclined towards the camera. A bird's nest, scraggly in the crook of a dogwood branch.

A picture of Zoe meeting her own gaze in the mirror. Over her shoulder stands Amy, the camera obscuring her face.

There is a picture of the plumes on the body of a flamingo that faces away. There are pictures of roadrunners, egrets, woodpeckers, buntings, owls. Killdeer, herons, swans. Cranes, turkeys, peacocks, ducks, geese, blackbirds, blue jays, crows, nuthatches, finches, martins, siskins, vultures, hummingbirds, hawks. The state bird of Oklahoma, the scissor-tailed flycatcher. A feather from a cedar waxwing between the pages of a book like a pressed flower; Amy recognizes the book, its squat Cyrillic letters, as the copy of Doctor Zhivago her father found her—not knowing what it was, perhaps just recognizing Amy's favorite letter, the butterfly, ж—when she was thirteen.

There is a portrait of a goat glancing up at the camera. Dozens of pictures from when the monarchs came to Minnesota in the summer after Amy's sophomore year: monarchs aloft, monarchs alit on fuzzy light purple-pink thistle buds. Their wings are tissue paper and stained glass, prominent white dots like glints of sun on water. There is a picture of a pelican looking into a lake sprinkled with raindrops, a picture of Zoe blowing a kiss from the couch in the living room, a silver ring on one slim finger. A picture of Zoe sitting beside a rosebush, gazing down at a rose whose perfect outline falls in shadow along the underside of her bare right arm.

There is a picture of Zoe leaping around above a sidewalk; a picture of Zoe shielding her eyes from the sun; a picture of Zoe sleeping on her stomach with her face pressed into the pale blue sheets; a portrait of a bumblebee in a geranium; a portrait of a black-and-blue moth on gray wood siding; a picture of a rabbit in a sea of bright green grass; a picture of three fat ostrich eggs at two sharp-taloned feet, the underside of a beak swooping in from the side; a portrait of a doe with her ears pricked up; a picture of a rusty Coke can on the riverbank, faded from red to pink; a portrait of a zebra on a carousel; a portrait of Zoe in a field of black-eyed Susans from the far side of the meadow at camp; a portrait of an ugly baby bird in brown leaves with a single green shoot of something standing straight up in the middle; a portrait of Zoe with her leg up on the bench before her like she's just hurt it, looking like she might cry, labeled in the perfect round letters of Amy's girlhood: Waluhili, June, 1995.

Once she's made three neat shining rows of images she takes a big step back. And now, as she surveys her pictures—each so balanced and so beautifully framed—it dawns on her, first, that every picture she has ever taken has been a portrait, and, second, that every portrait is a portrait of Zoe.

Every picture is a portrait of Zoe because Amy's intentions as a photographer have never wavered, although she herself had never known of them till now

What she wants—what she's always wanted—is to capture and to fix forever the presence of her sister, to contain her, to never let her go, or break, or even change. Whatever animal or bird, whatever butterfly or flower, whatever street, whatever car, whatever house has captured her eye, it has only done so insofar as it has featured some component of Zoe—some mood, some shape, some angle, some quality of glance. There were never really any action shots. And that seamless series of gestures that Amy performs, cradling the camera in her left hand, is always that same gesture: an attempt at a hermetic, time-repellent embrace.

Oh Zoe. If being homesick means I miss you,
then I guess I always have been.

The sun's still low on the horizon when she's done

As she nears the street, a truck pulls up, a German flag affixed to its antenna, Berliner Pilsner on its evergreen side. On the dashboard a vanity plate that says SASCHA, like that, in all caps, and with a C.

On her way to the train station, Amy stops at the post office, and just like that, she lets her sister go.

The next morning, in Paris, Amy goes to a café and orders un café crème s'il vous plaît. It makes her happy to say crème, because of how the r sounds and because she likes to think of the e's backward accent mark, a little gymnast. The tiny roof over the i in plaît.

When it comes she puts as much sugar in it as it can possibly hold—an old habit she's never bothered to break. Then she picks her cup up, gazes out across its snow-white cap as its perimeter comes undone from the ceramic in tiny almost imperceptible pops that turn it iridescent brownish gray. When she's ready, Amy fits the cup back into its groove on its saucer, relishing the sound.

Then she slips in her headphones and gives Zoe a call.

Zoe says, Oh hey, Sister, as though it's been fifteen minutes, instead of months, since they last spoke.

Hey, says Amy, clearing her throat, releasing her shoulders. What do you think Sasha would be doing now, if he were still alive?

There is a silence, and Amy regrets her question, thinking of course her sister doesn't want to play If Sasha Were. But then Zoe says, Probably something crappy, I guess, like accounting or shrubbery or something.

Amy's so surprised she snorts instead of laughing. Shrubbery? she says. Yeah, says Zoe, you know, like gardening or whatever. Shrubs.

The last portrait Amy takes of her sister is a picture of some hot-pink letters on the thick transparent railing of the Pont des Arts

Amy and Javi and Zoe are ambling from the Louvre to the Left Bank. Zoe's health is reasonably good right now, although she is in pain and still has little seizures, along with strange, fiery, snakelike sensations that course through her veins. It is Sunday; it is summer. Glints and reflections scatter out along the Seine. Amy glances back and says, Wait, in English, and then she switches: J'ai juste une petite chose à faire.

Zoe and Javi draw to a pause as Amy removes her camera from its case. Cradling it in her left hand, she takes a deep breath, studies her subject, and then, very gently, she presses the shutter button down.

Acknowledgments

No part of this project would have been possible without the eternal loveliness and grace and wisdom of Maxine Swann.

I am more grateful than I can ever say to the friends who read drafts and provided support throughout this long process: Stanley Simon Bill, Allison Bradley, Ginger Buswell, Ali Christy, Ellen Elias-Bursac, Laura Ginsberg, Colin Jackson, Bill Jacobson, Nathan Jeffers, Melissa Kitson, Bill Martin, Ben Merriman, Carolyn Purnell, Elisabeth Ross.

Lisa Ubelaker Andrade's brilliant insights have consistently enriched both this book and my life.

My patient, wildly talented partner, Boris Dralyuk, wrote the translation of Yevgeny Yevtushenko's poem that inspires Amy to brave new worlds. He has consistently given me courage, perspective and the extraordinary happiness of a home.

Thanks to my family for their unconditional encouragement and to Miklos and Gyula Gosztonyi and Nora Insúa for theirs.

Thank you to my brother Jay for coming to visit me in the hospital, and for always showing me kindness.

The pictures of me and of me and my sister, Anne Marie, and some of the earliest photographs of Anne Marie alone were taken by my mother, Laurie Croft. The letters pictured near the beginning of the book ("Or where they might be going?") are by the artist Jeffry Mitchell.

Corine Tachtiris has brainstormed with me about every endeavor I've ever undertaken, and I don't know what I would have done without her over the many years.

Thanks to my mentors, especially Lars Engle at the University of Tulsa and Clare Cavanagh and Samuel Weber at Northwestern.

Thank you to the MacDowell Colony, for giving me the space, time and inspiration to flourish.

My agent, Katie Grimm, has been this book's truest friend and most unflagging supporter. And my infinite thanks to my editor, Olivia Taylor Smith, for being intrepid and generous and helping *Homesick* to find its place in the world.

Thanks, too, to Eitán Futuro, *Homesick*'s muse.

АРАЛ МОРЕ.
L'EAU N'OUBLIE PAS
SON CHEMIN..!
©2011.